The Caregiver's Tale

# The Caregiver's Tale

*Loss and Renewal in Memoirs of Family Life*

## ANN BURACK-WEISS

 COLUMBIA UNIVERSITY PRESS    NEW YORK

Columbia University Press
*Publisher's Since 1893*
New York   Chichester, West Sussex

Copyright © 2006 Columbia University Press
All rights reserved

Library of Congress Cataloging-in-Publication Data

Burack-Weiss, Ann.
   The caregivers tale : loss and renewal in memoirs of family life / Ann Burack-Weiss.
      p.   cm.
   Includes bibliographical references and index.
   ISBN 0-231-12158-x (alk. paper)—ISBN 0-231-12159-8 (alk. paper)
      1. Caregivers—Case studies.   2. Chronically ill—Home care—Case studies.
   3. Chronically ill—Family relationships—Case studies.   I. Title.

RA645.3.B86 2006
362'.0425—dc22

                                                              2005053776

∞ Columbia University Press books are printed on permanent and
durable acid-free paper. Printed in the United States of America

c 10 9 8 7 6 5 4 3 2 1
p 10 9 8 7 6 5 4 3 2 1

*To the memory of my parents,*
*Pauline Levinson Burack, 1908–1980*
*Robert Burack, 1903–1980*

# Contents

# Part 3. The Memoirs

# Acknowledgments

The stories we tell, and the ways that we tell them, are influenced by everyone we've ever known, and everything we've ever seen, heard, or read. What follows, then, can be only an incomplete list of my indebtedness.

I am most grateful to the mothers, fathers, sons, daughters, sisters, brothers, life partners, and friends whose memoirs form the basis of this study. Without their books mine would not exist.

After close to four decades in the social work profession, I think back to all the stops along the way: Community Service Society, Jewish Home and Hospital, Gay Men's Health Crisis (GMHC), Lighthouse International, Brookdale Center on Aging, and Columbia University School of Social Work. I have received more from clients than I ever gave, and learned more from students than I ever taught.

First-rate colleagues surrounded me at every turn. Among them were a few who became dear friends: Frances Coyle Brennan, Gertrude Elowitz, Lucy Rosengarten, Barbara Silverstone, Anna (Honey) Zimmer. As the years pass, many who offered wise counsel are gone. I think especially of Daniel Cohen, Rose Goldstein, and Carol H. Meyer—I hear their voices still. Special thanks are due to Harriet Rzetelny, whose insightful comments on early drafts of the book helped immeasurably.

John Michel, at Columbia University Press, was the first person to whom I confided the nascent idea for what was to become my "project." Although he did not live to see it to fruition, his initial encouragement made all the difference. Shelley Reinhardt's good cheer and diligence—with the support of manuscript editors Kerri Sullivan and Susan Pensak—got me through the end zone.

Reading about other families brought me closer to my own. I honor my roots: grandmothers Rose Tuck Levinson and Fannie Lander Burack, who were children of the nineteenth century. I treasure my branches: granddaughters Danielle Nelson and Jennie Rose Nelson, who are children of the twenty-first century. And to the adored trio who grace my own small chunk of space and time in the universe—children Donna Weiss Nelson and Kenneth Weiss, and husband Roy L. Weiss—my deepest thanks and love.

> And the end of all our exploring
> Will be to arrive where we started
> And know the place for the first time.
> —T. S. Eliot, "Little Gidding"

# Crystallized Love

Man survives because he cares and is cared for. . . . Civilization is, at least in part, a form of crystallized love.
—William Gaylin

It is said that books in process take on a life of their own—mystified authors following their characters wherever they lead, unsure of where they're headed until all is revealed on the final pages. But that is supposed to happen only in fiction. Little did I imagine when I began this project that its course would undergo such drastic revision before its end.

This was to be a book about the professional view of "family caregiving"—a continuation and amplification of a theme I had introduced in a 1995 article in *Social Work* entitled "The Caregiver's Memoir: A New Look at Family Support." In that article I argued that the quantitative research that marks the field (centered primarily as it is on the concepts of "stress" and "burden") fails to capture the complexity of the experience.[1] I suggested that looking backward—after time had distilled the significance of the event—could allow the person who had served as caregiver to uncover the thoughts and feelings that exist below the radar of scientific inquiry. And I cited excerpts from a few published book-length memoirs to prove my point.

It was a topic close to my heart. For thirty years I'd practiced clinical social work with ill and disabled people and their families. As daughter, wife, and mother, I'd been involved in family care myself. All that I'd experienced indicated that caregiving was not an intrusion on family life but an intrinsic part of it, a crucible in which the crux of relationships was revealed; an occasion not only of stress and burden, but of growth, possibility, and meaning. Over time, I'd come to see "independent living" as an oxymoron, and to accept interdependence as the underlying order of life. Every family I'd ever known had at least one story of care inextricably bound to its sense of identity. The years may have obscured or exaggerated the particulars but the essence remained. The depth, shading, and nuance that accompanied these stories were not to be found in the professional literature. Nor were answers to the questions that interested me most: How do family caregivers "keep on keeping on"? How do their views on family and on the meaning of life itself change over the course of caregiving? How can their hard-won wisdom be used to sustain others faced with the same challenges?

Using published memoirs as research texts seemed an obvious way to examine these questions. Authored by sons and daughters, spouses and life partners, parents and children, they provide reflective accounts of the experience of caring for ill and disabled family members. As a caregiver, I'd drawn strength from reading the words of those who had passed that way before me. (In the words of a dearly remembered English professor, they "spoke to my condition.") As a practitioner, I'd sometimes suggested reading memoirs to my clients. And, in the tradition of Robert Coles (1989), who used fiction to develop the "moral imagination" of medical students, I assigned memoirs to the social work interns in my graduate school classes.

So tethered to the empirical literature was I that it seemed right to devote a major portion of the book to its review and to a discussion of the ways in which memoirs validated or contradicted the dominant paradigm of stress and burden. It seemed at first that an analysis of child-care, peer-care, and parent-care relationships in thirty book-length memoirs would do the job. I had no intention of moving beyond comparison—much less developing an overarching theory—in the process.

Many of the memoirs I chose to read featured caregiving in the sense that clinicians and researchers use the word: hands-on help with personal and instrumental tasks of daily living undertaken by one family member on behalf of another—usually for a time-limited period—of greater or lesser duration—of illness or disability.[2] For it is generally understood—if not publicly acknowledged—that most of the people occupying hospital beds today will not "get well soon," as the greeting cards on the bureau command. Nor will they die just yet. They will get a little better and go home, get a lot worse and come back. Good days will follow bad days as energy and spirits wax and wane. Bad news will follow good news as diagnostic tests yield contradictory results and second and third opinions are solicited. And throughout this time—however long it may last—ill and disabled adults will depend on those closest to them for help with tasks they once performed independently. Or, in the case of young children, will require more parental assistance than is usual for their age.

I began to read. Memoirs that centered on the accepted definition of caregiving were most often about the care of individuals with whom the author lived or had daily contact—young children, spouses, or life partners. Cancer, HIV/AIDS, and developmental disabilities were amply represented. Tales of stress and burden, amplified by insights into previously unrecognized facets of the experience—they were exactly what I expected to find.

But what of the ones that did not fit this mold—and there were so many! Memoirs by children, parents, and siblings of adults who were mentally ill, addicted, or trauma survivors. Memoirs in which hands-on care was minimally or never mentioned. *When Bad Things Happen to Good People* has become a classic since its publication more than twenty years ago. According to the author, Rabbi Harold S. Kushner, the book is a response to personal tragedy: his eldest son's illness of progeria (rapid aging) and death at the age of fourteen. This experience is a subtext of the book, but actual mentions of the family's daily struggles are few. Was this a "caregiving memoir"? Julie Hilden knew that her mother was rapidly succumbing to Alzheimer's Disease but did not return home until it was too late to care for her. The title of her book, *The Bad Daughter*, reflects its content and the depth of her remorse. Was this a "caregiving memoir"?

Jean Starobinski wrote: "One would hardly have sufficient motive to write an autobiography had not some radical change occurred in his life—conversion, entry into a new life, the operation of Grace" (cited in Olney 1998, 272). Every one of the memoirs I read—even those in which the author had been estranged from the ailing family member up to and including the moment of death—attests the truth of that observation. Given the life-transforming meanings to be found in these unanticipated memoirs, it was impossible to eliminate them on the grounds that they didn't fit into an a priori category.

The memoirs piled up. Each week seemed to bring publication of another. I passed the thirtieth and didn't even notice. I held myself to one rule: to read each in one sitting. If I started at dawn, I would end by nightfall. If I started in the late afternoon, I'd be up until the next morning. By employing the "total immersion" technique of language learning I drove out of my mind all families but the one before me.[3]

The cumulative effect of so much vicarious grief was immense. The stories cast a pall over my days and haunted my nights. Although I had long ago discounted Kübler- Ross's (1969) "stages" of grief as unmindful of individual variation, I found myself fitting all too easily into them. I moved from denial (that this project would not spill over into my life) to anger (at the cruelty of fate and of people), to bargaining (just one memoir more and my sample will be complete), to mourning (recalling, amidst all the sorrow, examples of courage, even joy), and finally to acceptance (that as they told their individual stories, I could tell their collective one).

Although I had intended to focus only on care relationships, I soon found that care situations were just as significant in shaping the narratives. The stories of caring for a family member with cancer were remarkably similar across memoirs of parents, spouses, and adult children. And the same could be said for mental illness or HIV/AIDS. Clearly it would not be sufficient to confine my study to relationships—situations would have to be included. Soon I began to recognize that each author described a care situation that fit into one of three narrative forms—the U, the arrow, or the spiral. The U is the illness from which the family member returned, such as when the cancer has been in remission for so long that it is pronounced a cure. The arrow is the progressive illness with a fatal prognosis, such as dementia. The spiral is the situation in which losses are permanent but not life-threatening; such as the disability that is the aftermath of an accident. Unlike the U, where the family member is returned to his former self, or the arrow, where he is on a direct downward course, the spiral denotes a self reconstituted on a lower level of functioning.

Bruner (2002, 66) would not have been surprised at this realization: "all cultures provide presuppositions and perspectives about selfhood, rather like plot summaries or homilies for telling oneself or others about oneself." Each narrative form was as constricting and as liberating as a Bach fugue. Point and counterpoint. What was lost, what was found. Though surface differences were great, authors were suffering similar losses, creating similar meanings from the experience. I began to realize that identifying common stories was the same as identifying common meanings.

Moving from a consideration of "family caregiving" to one of "family caring," considering care situations as well as relationships, and concentrating on the "lost and found" made comparison with the empirical literature irrelevant if not impossible. The evaluation of memoir texts involved a different methodology entirely. And here I entered the realm of narrative analysis. The literature was unfamiliar, but the beliefs on which it based was not. I had heard thousands of stories from clients—always aware that they were selected from the many incidents of their lives and shaped in a way they hoped would explain them to themselves and to me. Their stories held many common elements (for example, the difficulties in receiving needed support from others); in short, they reflected cultural conditions inextricably linked to, if not responsible for, their personal troubles.

Still, I had much to learn. Narrative analysts consider memoirs a subset of "life writing," nonfiction approaches to depicting the human condition that—along with essays, diaries, autobiographies, and biographies—reflect the cultural context of the individual experience. The few analysts who focused on narratives of illness and disability commingled first-person and caregiver narratives. Their interest in illuminating what G. Thomas Couser (1997, 289) termed the "gratuitous collateral damage" that contributes to the problems of the afflicted in our society has led them to examination of myths, metaphors, stigma, and marginalization—and to an affirmation of the power of the personal voice in bearing witness.

Couser, Anne Hunsaker Hawkins (1993, 1999), and Arthur Frank (1995) broke ground in recognizing the value of memoirs and in limning their cultural significance. They discuss some of the same books I do and come to some of the same conclusions. However, my exclusive emphasis on family care across the lifespan and the way I chose to portray it influenced the books I selected and the lens through which I viewed them.

Deconstructing memoirs to uncover their commonalities is an essential part of narrative analysis. It comes at a price: the unique family constellation, the particularities of each situation, and the power of the authorial voice are lost. Yet how much of what I read could be taken at face value? I accepted a few facts as literally true: that the authors were indeed the persons named on the cover and pictured on the book jacket; that the photographs sprinkled through the text were of their families; that their relatives suffered from the illnesses and disabilities attributed to them; that the care experience they described was the truth as they saw it. The artifices they used to shape a readable narrative—particularly verbatim conversations and omissions—were, finally, not significant.

Leibowitz (1989, 230) wrote: "Moods and events blur, facts are forgotten, misremembered, distorted. Faced with these handicaps, the autobiographer substitutes surmises, daydreams, idealizations, enthusiasms, thematic designs. Through the potent magic of style, the solitary confinement of time and consciousness may be transcended, and autobiography becomes what Edwin Muir called a fable."

I began to think of memoirs of slavery, the Holocaust, the Depression. A microcosm of the event could be seen in each story, while each story illuminated the whole. Over time, historical data and personal testimony merged in the public consciousness—to create a unified understanding of the event. Clearly, that was my charge—not to question what "really happened" but to draw from its recollection a collective truth. The challenge was to find a framework that allowed the individual memoirs to breathe; that honored their particularities while recognizing all that was myth, fable, about our shared culture of family care in the first years of the twenty-first century. There was no such framework at hand.

I recalled and reread the following: "Every work of literature has both a situation and a story. The situation is the context or circumstance, sometimes the plot; the story is the emotional experience that preoccupies the writer: the insight, the wisdom, the thing one has come to say" (Gornick 2001, 13). What, exactly, was the thing I had "come to say?" That family care is not limited to time-limited, hands-on activity during a period of illness or disability (as the bulk of professional "family caregiving" literature suggests) but is an integral, ongoing part of family life. That in telling the story of their experience, family members create meanings out of the care they provide. That these individual meanings are constructed at the point where the idiosyncratic history of the family member joins with socially constructed meanings of the situation (illness or disability) and the relationship (parent-child, sibling or life partner, adult child–parent). That meanings refer not only to what was lost but also to what was found. That the memoir—portraying the author's relation to self and others over time—is a narrative form particularly suited to portraying the fragile, mutable nature of family bonds. And finally, that reading memoirs will enhance the understanding of both the general reader who is dealing with the situation herself and the professionals she turns to for help.

One might wonder, of course, how representative those who write published book-length memoirs of the family-care experience are of the legions who do not. In the statistical sense, not at all. Novelists, journalists, poets, clergy, academics, lawyers, physicians, and public figures—the authors are a cultural elite, possessing educational, social, and financial resources beyond the reach of most of their readers. Yet memoirs do not exist in the realm of science but in the realm of art—and are to be judged by the standards of art. This is not to say that they are all literary masterpieces, but only to say that the truth of their words lies not on the pages of the text but in the way it resonates with its readers. We read the words of a father mourning the death of his son, a wife who is battling with medical staff over the care of her husband, a daughter who is finding new ways to communicate with a mother beyond speech—and we *know* them to be true.

One problem: how was I to reflect that truth to those who had not read the books themselves? "It is clear that we do not *find* stories; we *make* stories. We retell our respondent's accounts through our analytic re-descriptions. . . . In this sense the story is always co-authored" (Mishler 1995, 90).

Four decades ago the anthropologist Claude Levi-Strauss (1966) adopted the term "bricolage" to describe how disparate approaches can be pieced together to solve a research problem. Weinstein and Weinstein (1991, 161) further defined this method as an "emergent construction" that can include tools, methods, and techniques tailored to meet the needs of the researcher.

My guiding metaphor was not one of a collagist but of a jeweler, creating settings in which the gems (the authors' own stories, own words) could be shown to best advantage. I wanted to honor the stories by intruding upon them as little as possible while at the same time stressing their common elements. And so my method of analysis and the outline of this book evolved.

Whatever narrative structure a memoir author chose, it soon became clear to me that each family-care situation, each family-care relationship had its overriding story. Dementia had its own story. Sibling care had its own story. This story transcended the particularities of each family to tell what I came to think of as what Muir would describe as the care "fable" of that particular experience. This had to be broad enough to include all the variations to be found, yet specific enough to mark the experience as different from all others of its class. After identifying the common story, I challenged my own blind spots by trying to prove myself wrong. I looked again at each of the memoirs of the section. Where were the exceptions to the rule? Under what circumstances did the story not hold? It was gratifying when this internal dialectic confirmed my original idea. However, it was more useful when it did not—leading to significant revisions.[4]

Of all the authors read, about one-third are visited again and again. Prototypical of a care situation or a care relationship and eloquently written, their words give voice to the experiences of the others. Their memoirs became the source of quotes that drive the story and the case examples that enliven its narrative. Memoirs abound in metaphor and apt turns of phrase. I used these as chapter titles and excerpts that introduced and punctuated each chapter.

Although the memoirs are readily available, it is doubtful that anyone would read them all. So I thought it particularly important to provide ample representation of the work on which my findings are based.

Part I, "Care Situations," is introduced by a discussion of the cultural context of illness and disability as well as an overview of elements that all care situations share. Four chapters follow this one, each focusing on a commonly occurring family-care situation: cancer, HIV/AIDS, mental illness/chemical dependence, and dementia.

Part II, "Care Relationships," is introduced by an overview of common thoughts, feelings, and issues arising out of family care juxtaposed against a handful of memoirs of friend care. This is followed by four chapters, each discussing a family relationship: parents caring for ill or disabled children, brothers and sisters caring for siblings, spouses or life partners caring for each other, adult children caring for parents.

Part III, "The Memoirs," is introduced by a discussion of memoir formats, this is followed by paragraph-long summaries of each memoir in the study. These reflect the unique characteristics of each book. The section concludes with a chart for quick identification of those care situations and family relationships that may be of particular interest to the reader.[5]

An epilogue summarizes the findings of the study. It includes a reflection on the authors' common journey through the family-care experience by identifying and describing ten steps along the way from loss to renewal, and by discussing the lessons that the authors pass on to their readers. It also considers implications for clinical practice and future research.

Family care is a universal experience, and this book was written for anyone who has cared for, is caring for, or expects to care for a seriously ill or disabled loved one. What professional citations there are arise from the stories themselves and my attempts to understand them better. In no way intended as a compendium of family care information, this book offers one vision of the experience—and an invitation for others to read the memoirs for themselves.

Gaylin (1976, 13) sees care giving and care receiving as the root of civilization, the intangible quality of love rendered visible in "crystallized" form. Crystal seems to be a solid white block, yet when turned this way and that it reveals a prism. The authors whose memoirs fill these pages have found the prism in the crystal—in the process revealing a rainbow of colors and possibilities.

# part 1
## Care Situations

Because of the elusive nature of disease, the name is often the only available emblem. Once accepted, specific names quickly come to dominate social reality. The flavor of the name can make a real difference in how the disease is perceived and acted on.
—David Shenk

# chapter 1
## Introduction
### "The Flavor of the Name"

If your son lies dying in hospice, does it matter if he suffers from cancer or AIDS? If your mother denies that she ever gave birth to you, does it matter whether she has Alzheimer's Disease or schizophrenia? In other words, what practical difference does a medical diagnosis make in the life of a suffering family member?

A case could be made for the lack of difference, for the inadequacy of any disease category to explain or contain the responses of family members. So much seems to do with the individuals involved and the history of their relationship. So little seems to do with the diagnostic label affixed to the medical chart.

A case could also be made for professional terminology making a profound difference. After her own experience with breast cancer, Susan Sontag (1978) uncovered many historical and literary metaphors, ranging from the religious ("cancer" seen as a punishment or retribution for bad deeds) to the psychological (a "cancer personality," said to result from internalized anger and a lack of self-love). When AIDS emerged a decade later, Sontag revisited the theme with increased fervor (1989). Arguing that metaphors place a cruel burden on patients who are already fighting for their lives, she pled for illness to be stripped of all its connotations and be seen simply for what it is—a malfunctioning of the physical body.

Larry Dossey (1991, 19) terms Sontag's view a "hopeless ideal" and points out its flaws: "We may tell ourselves that our illness is nothing more than an accidental, purposeless, random event, that it is simply a matter of our atoms and molecules just being themselves. But this denial of meaning is meaning in disguise: It can assure us, for example, right or wrong, that the illness was not our fault, that we were not responsible for it, that it 'just happened'—which can be a great consolation. Thus, negative meaning is extremely meaningful."

*Why Her, Why Now*, the title of Lon Elmer's memoir of caring for a wife with cancer, poses the age-old question. As Job's comforters looked to religious lore for an answer, family caregivers turn to their physicians. Yet even when medical diagnoses can be linked to a single cause—muscular dystrophy to a genetic defect, AIDS to infection with a virus—there is no telling why the gene has passed to one child in a family and not another, why one person becomes infected with HIV after a single contact and another remains virus-free after several exposures. And for most diseases there are multiple causes. Genetic predisposition, environmental influences, life choices—all of the above probably interacting in some yet-to-be-discovered way. In the absence of certainty, there is ample room for metaphors to take root.

As each family comes to its own understanding of what is responsible for the fate that has befallen them, they draw upon a larger cultural understanding of illness, what Shenk calls "the flavor of the name." Some medical diagnoses have come to be seen as "no fault." Parents may agonize over unknowingly passing on a defective gene to a child, but no one holds them responsible. Some medical diagnoses allow for partial blame. The fact that brain anomalies or chemical imbalances have been found in people suffering from mental illness has not quite taken their families off the hook. Then there are diagnoses that one has acquired on one's own, such as chemical dependence: whether it is seen as medical disease or moral weakness, hereditary trait or character flaw, belief in free will allows for some degree of personal responsibility to be assumed.

Little has changed since Sontag illuminated the metaphoric uses of illness. If anything, the rhetoric has intensified. Cancer and AIDS continue to resonate with nonmedical meanings. And increasingly we subscribe to the notion of a "war" on disease. The disease is seen as an alien force that is trying to take over the healthy body: patients, physicians, and researchers alike are engaged in battle in which the goal is eradication of the enemy. We wince to remember that once it was quite common to speak of "the deaf and dumb" or "idiot children." We are careful now to use vocabulary that separates individuals from the conditions that afflict them. By speaking of "people with disabilities" rather than "the disabled" we affirm the primacy of individuals and the areas of their personalities that are untouched by illness. Such a semantic restructuring is tacit recognition that the war on a health-related problem can, despite the best of intentions, become a war on the person who has it. It is also a recognition that health problems may feel very different from the inside than they look from the outside.

Arthur Kleinman (1988) differentiates between the "disease" as recognized by the physician and the "illness" as experienced by the patient, in this way illustrating that it is the meanings attached to the situation rather than the situation itself that determine how patients and caregivers will respond. Kleinman believes that although the illness experience is always culturally shaped, "expectations about how to behave when ill also differ owing to our unique individual biographies. So we can also say of illness experience that it is always distinctive" (5). Sharing this perspective is Harold Brody (1987, 5), who characterizes the histories of his patients as "sickness stories," observing that "suffering is produced, and alleviated, primarily by the meaning that one attributes to one's experience."

James Buchanan (1989) does not look to cultural expectations or individual life histories to uncover the meanings of disease. He believes that meanings emerge from the body itself, arguing that "each disease has a characteristic mark which distinguishes it from each and every other disease. Patients can actually feel, experience, and sense this signature of their disease without being able to give adequate explanations or reasons for possessing such intelligence" (1).

Virtually all of the literary, philosophical, and medical theorizing on the meaning of illness focuses on the patient. There is little recognition of the impact that the social construction of disease has on family members. The memoirs I've surveyed suggest that there is as much metaphoric resonance in the lives of family members as in those of patients. And moreover, the meanings that family members ascribe to the illness experience often differ from those of the patient.

Jerome Bruner (2002) believes that "narrative in all its forms is a dialectic between what was expected and what came to pass. For there to be a story, something unforeseen must happen. Story is enormously sensitive to whatever challenges our conception of the canonical" (p. 15).[1] Although authors differ in where they begin their story, they all write of the time that separated before (when family life went on as it always had) and after (when awareness of the problem is first felt). Even when the patient is advanced in years, even when a physician might consider the situation far from rare, family members are initially surprised.

Perhaps this is why so many authors take time to get mobilized—initially denying the severity of the problem or expecting it to go away on its own. When the reality is finally recognized, they begin the search for answers. Shared plot lines, locale, and characters reflect a commonality that is discernible through a welter of flashbacks and digressions. They are introduced to a plethora of new people, institutions, and terminology. They come home with all the conflicting and troubling information and try to make sense of it. The body and mind of the patient may act and react in unaccustomed ways. Family members are uncertain what of past life can remain unchanged and what will be irrevocably altered.

Then the settling in—achievement of a new equilibrium and finding new ways of coping. This period may go on for days, months, years, or decades. The roller coaster analogy is frequently invoked. The ups and downs of the journey are described in detail—particularly the difficulty of making decisions in the face of conflicting medical opinions and a set of care options that is less than ideal. What course of action should be taken? Is the patient cognitively and emotionally capable of deciding for himself? And if (as is often the case) the patient is permanently or temporarily unable to understand his choices, how much risk is the family member willing to assume? There may be plateaus when everything seems under control, but these are invariably short-lived. Authors find, discard, re-find sources of concrete aid and emotional support. They keep on keeping on.

Although there are many positive endings—successful treatments for a range of physical and mental diseases are, thankfully, more prevalent every year—memoirs often end with the death of the patient (sudden or lingering, painful or peaceful), mourning, and the effort to find meaning in the experience—through its ordering and telling in memoir.

If the family-care narrative were a play, a minimum of sets would be needed. The patient's home—altered from its usual aspect by new uses for familiar objects (the coffee table covered by a tray of medicines) and the intrusion of alien objects (the hospital bed, the wheelchair, the rehabilitation devices). The hospital with its initialed frightchambers—the ER, the OR, the ICU. And The Waiting Room, where the minutes feel like hours as family members wait—for those who come and go, for what will happen next. Waiting rooms—whether in medical or rehabilitation centers—are the caregiver's natural habitat. Then there are the offices—offices that look like offices and offices in disguise: the living room for group meetings, the workplace for job training, the classroom for special needs—"congregate" settings where specially equipped vehicles take patients to socialization and training. Rooms redolent of the emotions lived within their walls.

The characters in the caregiver's narrative are divided between those who are paid to care (health care and social service providers of varying ranks and responsibilities) and those who aren't (family, friends, colleagues, neighbors).[2]

Many of the memoirs describe caring situations that require close and constant interaction with physicians: testing, hospitalizations, and high-tech interventions form the backdrop of these stories. (Cancer and HIV/AIDS are two of these situations.) But many more describe a care situation in which interaction with physicians is limited to initial diagnosis, monitoring, and crisis situations. (Chronic diseases, developmental disabilities, and Alzheimer's Disease among them.) Nevertheless, physicians figure prominently in stories of family care; their importance is less related to the frequency of their appearance than to its significance.

Some authors draw verbal portraits—often caricatures—of the doctors they encountered. Others ponder the dynamics of the relationship they have with them. But all share the same wish: to have their loved ones and themselves "seen" in all their human complexity; to be recognized as individuals rather than forgettable names on a medical chart. In the rare instances when this wish is fulfilled, authors describe the circumstances at length. Overtly songs of acknowledgment and homage, they bear a subtext of pride at being selected for a busy doctor's special consideration. The most notable men in their field drop everything to come to the care of John Gunther's son. Hillary Johnson's mother has a doctor who not only makes home visits but enjoys the family's company so much he stays on to chat. Janice Burns and her husband share a doctor who becomes a personal friend.

More often, authors feel they have to fight for every moment of time they receive. Molly Haskell—whose husband was hospitalized for months rapidly deteriorating from a condition that had not yet been diagnosed—likens the situation to that of children trying to capture the attention of distracted parents: "Like children, we compensate for our powerlessness by being shrewd manipulators. Instinctively, we try to ferret out and play on a doctor's vulnerability, present ourselves in a manner calculated to endear or, failing that, intimidate" (*Love and Other Infectious Diseases*, 29).

Another word for what Haskell sees as "manipulation" is coping—and the authors bring all that they can muster to their interactions with doctors. They promote easier access by making friends with the office staff. They rearrange their lives and schedules to fit into the life and schedule of the doctor. They swallow their anger and rationalize that it is the expertise that matters. They find few doctors who are incompetent. Although some may make mistakes in diagnosis and treatment, patients and families are generally charitable in their appraisals: they accept that medicine is not an exact science and that much is unknown. Not so with the emotional and psychological aspects of the situation. Here the authors cite example after example of arrogance and insensitivity. They write of receiving hasty explanations in darkened rooms, being allowed only one minute to grasp the message of the X-ray or the medical diagnosis (skills which, more than one author notes, took the doctors years to master). Almost as often, they are subject to what Karen Brennan, the mother of a brain-injured daughter, called "more information than we could bear." Jean Craig will never forget the doctor who didn't think it worthwhile to identify the source of an infection that was troubling her husband because he was "terminal" and would die soon anyway. Alan Shapiro will never forget the doctor who chose the moment that family members had stepped out of the hospital room to pressure his sister—whose judgment was addled by pain killers—to make a crucial treatment decision. These cuts are deep and the scar outlasts the life of the patient.

There are other health care professionals who appear on the scene at the time of diagnosis and beyond: therapists of every stripe, special education teachers, nutritionists, case managers, social workers, nurses, physical therapists. Putting together a plan that coordinates the contributions of all these people and calibrating it to the changing needs of the patient is an ongoing task of those authors who assume primary responsibility for their family member's daily functioning.

Authors are generally laudatory of the allied professionals they meet along the way and go to great lengths to praise the balance of personal warmth and skill they encounter. Thanks to them, family members learn a new language ("infant stim"), new skills (injecting needles), and a realistic set of norms against which to measure progress. Over and over, the authors sing the praises of good people met along their journey—people they would never have known if not for the situation that befell them. Their emotional support and practical help are particularly valuable when medical situations stabilize and patients are sent home to live with the consequences of impaired functioning. (The struggle to pay for these services out of pocket or the difficulty in achieving third-party reimbursement features prominently in many family-care narratives.)

Of particular note is the crucial role played by helpers of no specific training, helpers for whom there are no performance expectations, helpers who—nevertheless—employ head and heart in their caring. These indispensable aides are often mentioned by name and their contributions are not only "above and beyond" expectations but fill a void that no one else can. Once-a-week cleaning women give up their other "days" to become round-the-clock health care aides to their employers' spouses and parents. Babysitters invent games to distract howling children from the pain of treatments. Decades of college students become "friends" to autistic and developmentally disabled adults and prove able to break through to them in ways that many of their family cannot.

Authors may be surprised at the turning away of the few people they thought they could depend upon. But there are others who come through in ways that they could never have anticipated. Neighbors who take care of the children after school. Friends who drop off heat-and-serve dinners. Church members who form a prayer circle. Even if their hours are few and their help is around the edges of the larger problem, the importance of their involvement grows in retrospect.

A curious fact: less than a handful of care situations account for the origin of over two-thirds of the memoirs. I wondered why. Why were there were so many memoirs on Alzheimer's Disease and none on diabetes? Were there some care situations in which "the flavor of the name" was more compelling than others? Did each care situation have a story that marked it as different from all others, a story that would be the same no matter what the family relationship of patient and author?[3]

I decided to analyze four commonly narrated situations that occurred in every family relationship: cancer, HIV/AIDS, dementia, and mental illness/chemical dependence. (Developmental delays and autism also had many memoirs, but they were confined to the child-care relationship.)

There are many types of cancer, many dementia-producing illnesses. Mental illness and chemical dependence are frequent, but not inevitable, partners. HIV does not always progress to full-blown AIDS. I expected that intra-diagnostic variations would make a difference, that the age and gender of the patient would make a difference, that the medical, technological, and social changes would mark recent experiences as different from those that came earlier. What I found was that differences within diagnoses, increased treatment options, and changes in the public discourse rippled the surface but that the story of each diagnosis maintained its essential character throughout.

I thought about the illness as metaphor debate: if and how the authors were influenced by the cultural metaphors around them, the presence or absence of inner promptings that place a "signature" on the process. I found evidence to support every theory. And something more: the fact that each medical diagnosis is an open door through which family members embark on a journey whose itinerary was mapped long before their arrival. As Shenk (2001) suggests, "the flavor of the name" influences the responses of professionals, patients, and family alike.

Whether it is simply a pill that "may slow the process" of Alzheimer's Disease or an arduous course of medical, surgical, and chemical treatments for cancer, the diagnosis does indeed make a difference. And it is the messages they receive from those who are paid to care—in dynamic interaction with all the others—that finally determine how a family understands the meaning of the disease. (As Shaw's protagonist Henry Higgins famously confided to Eliza Doolittle, "the difference between a lady and a flower girl is not how she behaves but how she is treated.")

Seeking headings for each discussion, I chose a title or quote from a memoir of that section that reflected its central theme, its dominant story. Only later did I realize that each quote was a metaphor—a metaphor given breadth and depth by the array of separate situations it described. These powerful images invite readers to reflect on the gift of cancer, the secret that is HIV/AIDS, the companion demons of mental illness and chemical dependence, the sense of everything crumbling that is dementia.

The dominant story is not the only story. (There will be readers who viewed cancer as an unremitting horror, and readers who had no difficulty sharing an HIV/AIDS diagnosis with the world.) The dominant story is, however, the principal story as described in the memoirs. Often counterintuitive, often challenging professional views on the situation, it is a story that maintains its essential elements across the range of family-care relationships.

# chapter 2

## Cancer

### "Cancer's Gift"

[A mother writes:] "He grew more tired. After a while he whispered, 'Do something for me? Leave a little early. Walk a few blocks and look at the sky. Walk in the world for me. . . .' I walked through the blue luminous city night which suddenly had the look of spring. I walked lightly, carefully, cherishing his gift. He is dying—yet he is giving me life. Look at the sky! For all the days you may live, look at the sky and never lose it. It is there. It will always be there, if only you can see."
—Doris Lund, *Eric*, 309

"Cancer" and "gift" would hardly seem to belong in the same sentence, yet they are linked constantly in memoirs of child, spouse, and parent care, hinted at in titles (*Cancer's Gift, Healing Lessons, Midstream: The Story of a Mother's Death and a Daughter's Renewal*) and in excerpts like the one above. Caring for a loved one with cancer uproots the authors from their daily lives, sets them off on a torturous path, and brings them home again with a renewed appreciation for life. How can this be?

A comparison with other care situations points to differences in the social construction of the illness that affect the author's perceptions. Cancer carries a "now or never" urgency. Unlike mental illness or chemical dependence, there is no blame. Unlike HIV/AIDS, there is no stigma. On the contrary, sympathy flows freely and taking a "time out" from the usual responsibilities of daily life is considered an appropriate response. Some authors take leaves from work. Some rely more heavily on a spouse or friends. Some become frequent fliers or move in with their loved ones during periods of acute need. For them, as for Hillary Johnson, time may be "cancer's only gift"—but it is one they seize and use to the fullest.

The trajectory of cancer determines the length of the "time out," typically scattered days and weeks throughout the course of treatment and intense involvement of a month or so at the end. Physically separating themselves from an accustomed routine means leaving the world of the well and entering the world of the sick. What starts out as a response to a patient's needs turns, unexpectedly, into a personal retreat for family members, a time to reflect on existential issues and reconsider the purpose of their lives.

The memoir authors experience cancer as a call to action. Family members put aside their differences and work together. Divorced parents and alienated siblings unite in arranging simple pleasures and marking special occasions. Friends of the patient and of the caregiver show up at just the moment they are needed. If patients are employed, they may rise a few levels at the workplace days before their death (for instance, Alan Shapiro's sister Beth receives a promotion to chief librarian, and Nancy Rossi's husband learns that he has achieved the coveted position of partner in his law firm). Whether their support is a one-time gesture or an ongoing commitment, cancer offers an opportunity for everyone who knows the patient to think well of themselves.

Yet all of this "feel good" activity takes place against a harrowing backdrop. Unlike memoirs of other illnesses, which often weave back and forth through time, cancer stories are essentially chronological. Pre-diagnosis recollections may be inserted here and there to individualize the patient and the relationship, but those events seem to have taken place in another universe. Periods of remission are brief, bittersweet interludes in cancer narratives—linking the ambiguity of diagnosis and initial treatments with the certainty of the terminal phase that concludes most memoirs.

In an alarming number of cases, cancer is initially misdiagnosed (the brain tumor of Philip Roth's father is diagnosed as Bell's Palsy;

LeAnne Schreiber's mother's gastrointestinal symptoms are first attributed to a "late-blooming milk allergy"; and even though Alan Shapiro's sister has a history of breast cancer, the metastasis of her condition is believed to be a sinus infection). The agony of hearing a dreaded diagnosis is thus exacerbated by its delay. Family members typically become involved during this phase—seeking out several medical opinions, and preparing themselves and their loved ones for the path ahead.

Even though the exact time of death cannot—and perhaps should not—be predicted, cancer patients and their families live in its shadow. But what do they know and when do they know it? How do they speak of it among themselves? There has been a sea change in attitudes toward cancer in the past two decades—a change that is reflected in the memoirs themselves. In *Staying Alive*, published in 2002, Janet Reibstein writes of breast cancer as experienced by her aunts, her mother, and herself. In her book, the empowering shift from being a "cancer victim" to "living with cancer" is graphically portrayed as each woman faces the situation at a different time and she and her family members respond in a different way.

It is striking, now, to read memoirs written before 1970, when the necessity for secrecy (rationalized in the name of maintaining hope) was unquestioningly accepted. Simone de Beauvoir's mother was never given the name of her illness. John Gunther maintained the pretense that his son, Johnny, was going off to Harvard in the fall even when it was clear that he would never leave his hospital bed. From a diary discovered after his death, it was evident that Johnny knew how ill he was but was maintaining the façade.

Where contemporary readers might see a lost opportunity for intimacy and comfort, John Gunther and the readers of his day saw courage. This changed after the 1969 publication of Elisabeth Kübler-Ross's *On Death and Dying*, a book that enjoyed wide popularity among both professionals and lay people.[1] She made a persuasive argument for the importance of everyone talking openly about the situation to those living through it; and in so doing, allowing them to express the feelings that society had long suppressed. Since that time, cancer has lost its association with certain death—largely due to the development of many successful treatments. Thus, changing prognoses as well as changing philosophies have contributed to the attitude of caregivers toward discussing the illness with their loved ones.

The accepted philosophy of today—that family members follow the patient's lead—is evident in most memoirs. Usually it is the patient in whom the ultimate responsibility for making decisions rests. While this can be agonizing for authors who have a different view, it is a relief of sorts. By following the patient's wishes they are relieved of a responsibility that few wish to assume.

Most authors describe themselves as virtually drowning in information about possible courses of action. These boil down to essentially three routes: the medical path, the alternative path, and the integrative or complementary path (a combination of medical and alternative approaches). The presence of three routes and multiple alternatives within each route can be overwhelming, but it is also comforting. Whatever road one chooses, there are success stories. If one treatment fails, a backup usually awaits. The hopefulness of cancer treatment, along with the busyness of mastering the concrete details, fills the family member and patient's time with shared, purposeful activity and a sense of control over their destinies.

Most families choose the route of traditional medicine—which can include surgery, chemotherapy, or radiation. Since these treatments are medically administered, the roles of patient and caregiver are to bear with them as best they can. On the traditional path, physicians are the star performers. When they are good, they are very good. Examples of their availability (they call back on weekends, they make house calls) and compassion (they offer precisely the needed words of comfort at just the right moment) are given. Far more space is accorded to physicians who lack this lauded human connection. Even when their professional competence is unquestioned (and most are acknowledged as knowing their business) they fail patients and families by not recognizing the psychological and social needs that accompany cancer treatment.

The traditional route is inherently infantilizing . Shapiro writes of his sister Beth: "She came to see her doctor as an all-knowing and all-powerful parent. Since her survival depended on his expertise, it was impossible for her not to invest that experience with almost magical potency. . . . Dr. P became not just her potential saviour but also her potential judge. More than anyone else, early and late in her disease, he determined how she felt about herself" (*Vigil*, 53).

An exclusively medical model is followed unquestioningly in memoirs dating before 1990; after that time it is most often followed by parents making unilateral decisions for minor children and adult children making decisions conjointly with their aged parents. In the latter case, the son or daughter's role ranges from information gathering and support to taking total responsibility for a parent who is unwilling or unable to grapple with the pros and cons of various courses of action. Thus, while Philip Roth accompanies his father to the specialist's office and sits quietly by as his father unfurls the list of questions he has prepared, it is he who adds the answers up to recognize that the least invasive treatment is the best alternative.

Consideration of alternative cancer therapies is found in the narratives of mid-life adults who came of age in the 1960s. Whether it is the wife or husband who is the patient, the spouse is generally an equal partner in the search for aid. They come across the same remedies (interferon, herbs, meditation, diet), listen to the same preachers (Stephen Levine, Bernie Siegel, Louise Hay), and share the same philosophy (that they have power and must take control of what is happening to their bodies).

Those who approach alternative methods as adjuncts rather than substitutes to traditional therapies are common. Those who totally eschew medical help, like Paul Linke's wife, Chex, are rare. It is only as she lies dying that she questions the decisions she made. Some friends are angry with Paul: Why did he go along with her? Couldn't he have insisted that she get medical help? But, secure in their division of labor, he has no regrets. Her job was to make the choices. His job was to help her carry them out.

Periods of respite (whether gaps in treatment or full-fledged remissions) are bright and shining interludes in cancer narratives. It is as if patient and caregiver stepped out of Thornton Wilder's *Our Town*—entering a world once taken for granted, now infused with clarity and significance. Every day, however ordinary, becomes precious. Sometimes new ventures are undertaken; sometimes old interests are returned to with renewed vigor. Stanley and Andrea Winawer take one memorable trip to Positano and another to Nice—visits that once would have been deferred indefinitely can be postponed no longer. Jean Craig and her husband, Ed, find their comfort in continuing to live as normally as possible. They buy a business, enjoy their home and family as if there were all the time in the world to do so.

The new intimacy that takes root at this time (and continues throughout the course of the illness) enables the veil of habit to fall away. The cancer patient and his family have time to see each other in a different light. Alan Shapiro goes so far as to speak of the joy that accompanied the family vigil at his sister's bedside: "Joy in the self-forgetfulness that came with tending Beth, with grieving for her, and in caring so tenderly for each other as we grieved; joy in the dissolution of the opaque privacies of daily life, in the heightened clarity of purpose and desire" (*Vigil*, 5).

Awareness of a foreshortened future imbues every experience with importance. Janet Farrington Graham, a devout Christian, finds herself side by side with her mother, their hands blackened by coins, working the slot machines at Las Vegas. Her mother will soon return home, to face more treatments and probably death. But for now she is doing what gives her the most pleasure in the world, and her daughter treasures the shared moments—all the more significant because they will not happen again.

Lon Elmer, who lived through cancer with his wife, describes her trajectory. It is a course borne out in many of the memoirs: "Ups and downs in which each up is lower than the one before it, followed by a plateau, a leveling off at a level recognizably higher than the ups immediately preceding it, then a swift decline to death" (*Why Her, Why Now*, 28). If the end is measured in days, it is usually "swift," but in terms of suffering, it seems to go on forever. Authors describe these days and weeks in detail. The hospital, the hospice, the bedroom filled with rented equipment. The reader is invited in: to inhale the stale air, empty the spittoon, find the bedpan too late. Minute by minute descriptions of the dying process commemorate the physicality of the struggle. The heavy breathing. The death rattle. The silence.

The thoughts after that silence. Thoughts that had much in common with Sidney Winawer's: "Our experience reordered our priorities. . . . We wanted to be that white-haired couple walking down the street holding hands, while people smiled to see us. What we learned was not to wait. We learned to take the moments that were given us" (*Healing Lessons*, 259).

# chapter 3
## Dementia
### "Everything Crumbles"

[A husband writes:] "In the beginning she had lost only nouns and episodes of long-term memory: the warned-of loss of recent memories soon followed. Then memories of how to make sentences, the sequence of days, how to put one foot in front of the other, intellection—everything crumbles, as in movies of rivers in flood, breaking through dikes, overrunning them, inundating the low ground except for random hummocks of refuge, and rising inexorably toward the once-safe house."

—Aaron Alterra, *The Caregiver*, 93

You've known them so well for so long that they have become a part of you. You don't need to wonder what he likes and dislikes, what arouses him to anger, what brings him joy. You've seen her meet many of life's challenges—perhaps she was even the one you turned to in your own times of trouble. If he were physically ill, you could talk with him about what should be done. If she died you could be warmed by her memory, mourn all that she was, and move on. But the doctor pronounces him fit as a fiddle and she has not died; in fact, she is pacing up and down in front of you right now asking—for the twentieth time in five minutes—"When are we going?"

Who has watched one of the many versions of the science fiction film *Invasion of the Body Snatchers* without a visceral understanding that it reflects one of our deepest fears—not that pod people will invade the earth, but that people we know as well as we know our- selves, people who continue to look exactly like they always did, could change *inside*. And these changes would not be just in relation to the world at large but in relation to us. He could look at us without seeing us. We could no longer see ourselves reflected in her eyes.

Retrogenesis is what it's called: a benign term until we realize its literal definition, "a return to the beginning." The personality of the patient erodes as it developed—sometimes in sharp spurts, some- times in stages that blend imperceptibly into one another. The slope may be gentle or steep, the plateaus may be wide or narrow, but the destination is never in doubt. The trip back is not a generic journey. Just as babies show their individual natures at birth, so sufferers may retain aspects of their personality until close to the end. Alzheimer's Disease, multi-infarct dementia, organic brain diseases, strokes—all cause irreversible losses of the spouse or parent who once was.

For some memoir authors, the onset is dramatic. Marion Roach's mother inexplicably scooped up her beloved cats and took them to the vet to be put away. Charles Pierce's father set off in the car on a short errand and was found the next day parked on a street many miles away with no idea of how he got there. However, for most care- givers the awareness that something is wrong dawns slowly—not in a single incident but in a series of small observations. When a family member has periods of forgetfulness and disorientation that coex- ist with usual functioning, it may take some time to recognize that something is wrong and to seek professional confirmation. This is especially the case when the patient is relatively young or there are alternative medical explanations for the condition (as in the situation of Beverly Bigtree Murphy's husband, who was believed to be suffer- ing from the aftermath of a car accident, and of many parents with a history of heavy alcohol use).

A majority of dementia memoirs chronicle the case of Alzheim- er's Disease—a diagnosis of exclusion of other neurological diseases, confirmed (as are the related disorders) by the ubiquitous mental status test. Drawing a clock face, counting backward from 100 by 7's, remembering three words after a short pause, stating the date, the season, and where the interview is taking place prove difficult even for those in the early stages. Looking on as a beloved spouse or parent struggles with the simple test is a pivotal event in the life of many of the authors. So it is not a matter of stubbornness or temporary distraction after all—it is a disease for which there is no cure. And it will most likely get worse. In the absence of accompanying physical conditions, Medicare and most insurance companies will not cover care. Families must find their way as best they can.

Preserving the dignity, individuality, and autonomy of the patient is a goal that is shared by all the memoir authors. The difficulty of converting these worthy ideals into action is their greatest heartache. The sufferer who is physically well and active poses the greatest challenge. If he is free to come and go as he pleases, he may wander off. If he continues to drive, he is a danger to himself or others. Home alone, he is capable of setting off a fire or flood. He may still be capable of independently caring for some personal needs. He may still sound like his old self at times. But continuous supervision—in his own home or in the home of an adult child—is soon necessary.

Marion Roach describes it thus: "It goes on and on, and just when we can't stand another phase, we don't have to, because it's succeeded by another one—a worst phase, a sloppier phase, a phase of hushed panic—seen in the eyes of the victim, seen by us. The one who knows best—the victim—about what is happening, loses the ability to tell us, the family, how to help. The ability to panic leaves the victim; it swarms over the family" (*Another Name for Madness*, 179).

It is at this point that most caregivers undertake a change in their lives. They manage to cobble together a plan that works, at least for a time. Care may be shared by members of the family, a day care program, and paid companions. (The Alzheimer's Association—and the many support programs it sponsors—is cited by many as a great help, especially in the difficult period following diagnosis. Some caregivers seek only information and resources, while others find a lifeline in the regular meetings of a mutual aid group.) It seems as if they will be able to manage after all. Until the time comes when they see that they can't.

Dealing with incontinence and confusion of night for day leaves the authors exhausted. Repetitive questioning and actions drive them to their wit's end. And they lash out in anger. In fact, the moment of uncontrollable anger is a pivotal point in many dementia narratives. It erupts without warning from the author, who believes he has everything—including his emotions—under tight control. Words of frustration, fatigue, disgust—a rain of rage let loose on a trembling, uncomprehending victim. The shame that follows an outburst of anger is immense. Sometimes it is presented as a rationale for the spouse or adult child to seek more help. More often it stands alone—a confession to the unknown reader. How can we not understand—and forgive them—more easily than they do themselves?

Authors who write of a loved one's dementia share moments of exquisite pain that mark the beginning of the end. Charles Pierce writes: "All at once, the light came back into my father's eyes, and his face changed. It arranged itself slowly into an expression of unspeakable sadness. He gripped my arm. His mouth began to move as though he were trying to choke something out to me. He began to cry with the effort he was making. He was there, floating in front of me for a moment and then he was gone again. It was the last time I ever saw the person my father had been" (*Hard to Forget*, 46).

When the patients are well into the middle stages of dementia, authors strive to reconcile two images of their loved ones: who they once were and who they have become. Acceptance of an irrevocably diminished parent does not happen after a single incident: there are usually several trials to restore the person to himself. The occasion when the authors finally accept that the family member they remember will not return is often described in poignant detail. Sue Miller purchases a series of symphony tickets for her confused father, concerned only that difficulty differentiating between the end of a piece and the end of a movement might lead to inappropriate clapping and embarrassment. When he wanders out of the concert hall at intermission and is missing for a lengthy and frightening period of time, the reality of his condition can no longer be denied.

When the patient can no longer consistently recognize his surroundings or the people in them, when the day-to-day difficulty of care becomes overwhelming, when financial resources are exhausted, most adult children reluctantly concede that a nursing home (whose cost can be assumed by the government) is the only alternative. Spouses hang on longer. Yet the time comes for them as well.

The nursing home experience—described in detail in most of the memoirs in this section—may be far from perfect, but it usually marks an improvement. Frequent visits, the celebration of birthdays and holidays, taking the mother or father who is now a "resident" out for meals, rides, or family visits (on which he invariably expresses the wish to return to what has now become home) are continued as long as feasible.

Relations with the para-professionals who care for the demented family member—whether home health care workers or nursing home staff—is under constant negotiation. There is the usual array of those who care with exquisite sensitivity, those who are brusque and uninterested, and the majority who do their job competently. Occasionally, there are blowups. Despite assurances of safety for "wanderers," Brenda Avadian's father is able to walk out of a nursing home his first night there. Reluctant to admit that they were at fault, the administrators say that he is beyond their capacity to manage and suggest that she take him home. Observing that the overall care is good and that she can work with them on difficulties as they arise, Avadian insists on his continuance. And is gratified to find her initial beliefs justified.

Memoirs of dementia teem with discussion of the outside help caregivers were able to obtain: how much, how good, with what consequences. In fact, assistance with physical care emerges as a crucial determinant of how well the author copes with the emotional demands. For the key emotional task of dementia care—accepting that the person you once knew is gone and learning to find a new humanity in the person who is now in his place—is impossible while old expectations are maintained. Spilled food and bathroom messes can be overlooked if you are not the one who has to clean them up. When expectations die, along with blame of the patient for not meeting them, authors are freed to form new relationships with their own rewards.

As the disease progresses, they find satisfaction if they observe the basics of keeping the patient clean, dry, and fed being performed with skill and tenderness. They no longer cringe when they observe the patient finding comfort and delight in childhood pleasures: stuffed animals, colorful cartoons, sweet foods. They do not need to talk constantly to fill the vacuum, but are able to sit in patient silence.

The end of Alzheimer's Disease and many related causes of dementia is a shutting down of the body functions leading to death. Because so much has already been lost by the patient, the end is seen by most authors as a relief. Yet they often wish they could have held on longer, done more. Diminished financially (sometimes drained physically and emotionally as well), they are rightfully angry at the lack of emotional and governmental support. They often wonder how things could have been different if money and time and strength were no object. What if one could design the perfect setting? Hire the perfect attendants? Devote a major portion of one's life to care for the afflicted spouse or parent?

The experience of Reeve Lindbergh is unique among caregivers in that all of these conditions were possible. When her ninety-three-year-old mother, the renowned Anne Morrow Lindbergh, suffered dementia following a number of small strokes, all could be arranged. A specially designed house with a beautiful view, filled with the treasures of a lifetime, right next door to a devoted daughter. Round-the-clock teams of skilled and loving attendants—exquisitely sensitive to her former tastes (when she cannot sleep at night, they read to her from Rilke). She is beautifully groomed and dressed, receives daily visits from friends, family members, and every provider of health care or personal services imaginable. She is surrounded by love, by wonderful things to look at, to touch, to hear. It all works for a time. Then she stops speaking.

Painful though it is at first, Lindbergh learns to live without her mother's words. She learns that sitting together in silence is a powerful communion. She forms a new relationship with "this vestigial, wraithlike Other Mother." And when this Other Mother continues to fade and ultimately dies—a process that bears an uncanny resemblance to those for whom retrogenesis wreaks its havoc in less enviable surroundings—she is ultimately at peace. As many adult children and spouses before her, Lindbergh reclaims and is comforted by memories of the person her mother once was: "Her quiet voice, her exquisite gentle articulation, her loving eloquence, all of these things spoke to me through my days, comforted my nights, and gave each hour of every twenty-four its substance, shape, and meaning from the time that I was born" (*No More Words*, 15).

# chapter 4
## HIV/AIDS
### "Burden of a Secret"

[A grandfather writes:] "Lying goes against my Christian character and my personal integrity. Moreover, I soon discovered that I did not have to tell everything I knew about our family's situation to make it through most conversations. In answer to questions about Bryan's condition as well as Matt's, I could honestly reply, 'He has awful congestion in his chest,' or 'He has a problem with his blood,' or 'He has a respiratory disorder,' or 'His resistance is extremely low.' All of these descriptions, of course, were symptoms of AIDS but most people's curiosity was satisfied with a surface explanation. As such we were able to maintain the secret without violating our personal principles."
—Jimmy Allen, *Burden of a Secret*, 73–74

Imagine awakening one day to a world turned upside down: the truths you've lived by revealed as lies, the people you relied upon turning away, the doors of church, school, and hospital—wide open to others—only reluctantly held ajar for you. And leaning on you for support is a loved one suffering from a disease about which little is known beyond the fact that it is fatal. If that is not enough to throw you into a state of disequilibrium and despair, imagine that you too have the disease and the one dependent upon you is your life partner or your child.

All of the HIV/AIDS memoirs included here describe care experiences that took place between the mid-1980s and the mid-1990s. The first thing to be said about these experiences is that things are different now. That decade spanned a time when most of the people who carried the virus were not aware of it until they became seriously ill. A time when diagnosis meant that death was rarely more than a year away. A time when fear of contagion through casual contact ran high (despite mounting medical evidence that "at risk" behaviors were few and known). A time before blood banks routinely screened for HIV. A time when mother-to-child transmission was common. A time before HAART (highly active anti-retroviral therapy) held the promise of treating AIDS as a chronic manageable disease.

The second thing to be said about these experiences is that things are, in many ways, the same. It is true that blood transfusions are no longer a threat, mother-to-child transmission can be prevented, and unfounded fears of contamination have been laid to rest. But there is not yet a vaccine. There is not yet a cure. There are still new infections. And while medications have significantly extended the life expectancy and years of good functioning of may people living with HIV, some strains of the virus prove resistant to all interventions. People are still dying.

Most intractable and enduring is the profound stigma of the diagnosis itself—which is due to the fact that HIV/AIDS is often contracted through culturally disapproved behaviors such as IV drug use and homosexual sex. As current experiences in Africa and Asia attest, however, the diagnosis carries such negative power that even monogamous married women who contracted the virus from their husbands are treated as outcasts.

In naming his memoir *Burden of a Secret* Jimmy Allen captures the essence of the HIV/AIDS journey, as true today as it was at the beginning of the epidemic. Stigma breeds secrets. Secrets within secrets, like a nest of Russian dolls—uncover one and another lies waiting. And stigma and secrets affect the authors of the narratives as surely as they do the patients for whom they care.

Disclosure is a crucial issue for many. Allen fears his grandsons will be discriminated against at school if the cause of their many illnesses becomes known. Elizabeth Glaser, herself infected with the virus, has the same fears for her infected son and daughter. Even Elizabeth Cox, who is virus free, believes that fear engendered by her husband's status will spill over to their uninfected son. These caregivers find compromises that satisfy their own sense of responsibility while not sacrificing their children. Yet crafting and maintaining the secret is a huge expenditure of energy and worry.

There is another kind of secret that rocks authors to the depths of their beings: suddenly learning that the loved one they thought they knew was another person entirely. It is only when her husband becomes ill that Elizabeth Cox finds out that not only has he been unfaithful, but that the adultery took place with another man. It is only when her father becomes ill that Susan Bergman sees that his persona as a churchgoing husband and father of four is a sham beneath which lies a hidden homosexual life.

Then there are the secrets that caregivers have not yet faced about themselves. The early lives of Jamaica Kincaid and Barbara Lazear Ascher have little in common. Kincaid, who is of African descent, has fled the rural Antigua of her birth to reinvent herself in America. In so doing, she consciously separated herself from her family and community. Ascher unquestioningly carried on the suburban Caucasian middle-class life of her parents. Both women are now wives and mothers involved in their own lives. If they live at a considerable distance from their younger brothers and see them infrequently, it is not a source of regret. Ascher is uncomfortable around the flamboyant theatricality of her openly gay brother, Bobby, while Kincaid's brother, Devon, is part of the island life she escaped.

AIDS changes everything. It is not that physical closeness is reestablished (although the sisters arrange for more frequent visits—and Kincaid expends great cost and effort in getting the latest drugs to Antigua—they still have lives apart). Rather, AIDS forces both sisters to question themselves: their attitudes toward their brothers' sexuality, and regrets over a past that cannot be undone. A large portion of both memoirs is devoted to the unexpected grief that floods over them after their brothers have died.

Anger is endemic in memoirs of AIDS care—and its manifestations range from the intensely personal to the globally political. Elizabeth Cox characterizes her husband's homosexual encounter as "sordid" and attributes his participation to childhood sexual abuse (as if only trauma could explain a same-sex attraction). Marion Winik knew her husband was gay when she married him, knew that he had a problem with drugs when she introduced him to heroin; still she faults him for reverting to old behavior after he is diagnosed. Susan Bergman is scathing in her descriptions of her skeletal father's attempts at physical attractiveness. Jimmy Allen tells his gay son that although he loves him he cannot offer "acceptance" because he practices behavior that is condemned in the Bible.

"These men are sick unto death," the reader might think. "Enough!" Then reconsider. Cox and Bergman have been betrayed. Not only is their present and future affected—all of the past is called into question, each pleasant memory tainted by new knowledge. Winik is in recovery and seeks to protect their two sons. As for Allen, the Bible is the very core of his existence; to deny its teaching is to lose all sense of his own identity. These family members do not run. They stay and they care and they love—not "because" but "even though."

Writing of her decision to care for a friend, Amy Hoffman notes, "With the virus, you make a choice. When someone gets sick, you're either in or out. That's it. No middle ground" (*Hospital Time*, 15). Notwithstanding that choice, Hoffman questions her own reactions. "I hated myself during the era of Michael's sickness. I pushed myself into the middle of it, and then I not only resented him and his needs and his crazy demands, but I also became jealous of anyone else who took care of him, who stopped in for a visit even. I wanted to be better than all of them. And I was worse. People would say, 'you're so wonderful to do so much for him,' and I'd feel they'd exposed my hypocrisy" (9).

For most of the authors in this section, simply writing their stories was a political act. They showed pictures. They named names. In breaking the bonds of secrecy, they made it easier for those who come after them. Many went further. Elisabeth Glaser set up a foundation for pediatric AIDS. Hydeia Broadbent and Janice Burns put a face on the epidemic by becoming official spokespersons. Fenton Johnson, Paul Monette, and Edmund White wrote luminous love stories and so challenged many societal stereotypes of gay relationships.

In the decade covered by these memoirs about HIV/AIDS the course of the illness was brutish and short. Information was minimal, medical options were few, and a great deal of trial and error marked the treatment process. Many physicians were seen as helpful and concerned. When she learns that Allen's grandchildren were being shut out of activities, their doctor brings her own children to play with them and makes sure that pictures of their time together are widely shown. The dedication of a self-selected band of early physicians was not matched by all of the health-care team, however. Some surgeons refuse to operate on people with HIV. And even when nurses were not frightened, they lacked understanding of common symptoms.

Religious institutions come up for the greatest criticism. Although Allen was a leader in the Southern Baptist church, colleagues turned away when he asked them to admit his family, fearing that they would lose parishioners if they become known as an "AIDS church." Cox's husband was in the hospital when he was approached by a nun who "asked him what kind of prayer she would like her to say for him. Keith asked for a hopeful prayer. She said it was hard to find a hopeful prayer for patients with AIDS" (*Thanksgiving*, 156).

The end stage of AIDS is physically reminiscent of cancer. The emotional climate is fraught with the same angst that characterizes the entire illness. There are hospital deaths and hospice deaths and home deaths. Few patients take matters into their own hands (Cox's husband says goodbye to everyone, then takes the medication he has stockpiled). Most let the illness take its course. Palliative measures are in short supply, and the suffering is beyond belief.

There is a notable exception to the anger, the ambivalence, and the secrets—the case of gay partners: Fenton Johnson, Paul Monette, Edmund White are clear in their expectations. If their lovers' families wished to become involved in care, they had to accept their child's homosexuality, HIV status, and the relationship itself. Sometimes family and lover worked the relationship out harmoniously, but just as often there was a degree of reservation that hurt all the more for its veiled expression.

Monette and White were themselves infected with the virus. They and their partners had a committed relationship before learning of their status. Seeing a lover grow ill and die was thus a portent of their own future. Johnson faced a different situation: "When I told people I had a lover who had AIDS, I heard in their voices the assumption they leapt to; that I myself must be HIV-positive, that I myself must be on the verge of death, because why else would I stick with a man dying of a communicable disease? Each time I felt defensive, torn between the urge to say, 'Oh, but I'm HIV-negative' and feeling that it was none of their damned business; that their place was to educate themselves in the workings both of HIV and of love" (*Geography of the Heart*, 169).

"The workings both of HIV and of love" are intertwined in these memoirs. For gay men, sharing their HIV status often recalls an earlier time when they struggled with rejection after "coming out" as homosexuals. But time has passed and these authors know better than to let the meaning of their relationships be defined by others. In speaking of their past—and of the illness itself—they note the injustices and slights but do not dwell on them. Rather they memorialize their lives together. The trips away, the mementos collected, the private celebrations at home, all serve to celebrate the preciousness of the shared moments—all now treasured memories.

If you are not in the habit of reading book introductions, and miss the telltale sentence here and there, you could classify *Our Paris* as a charming recollection of a time and place: droll illustrations and a rambling text about the experiences of a carefree couple and their dog, Fred, as they make their way through a strange and wonderful world. Edmund White wrote the text. His lover, Hubert Sorin, did the artwork. The introduction is written on the very day that Sorin died. Edmund White explains, "It was our undoubtedly absurd notion of gallantry that made us pretend (in his drawings) that his body was not aging and wasting away or (in my chapters) that we had nothing more serious to do than loaf in the streets and give dinner parties. All bluff, since toward the end we seldom saw anyone or went anywhere. Hubert came to despise his emaciated body but in his drawings he remains as dapper and handsome and élancé as he was the day I met him, five years ago," and although in the last months the dog must be given to a brother because "I couldn't take care of both Hubert and Fred," "in our book we remain an eternal trio, our silhouettes against the Tour St.-Jacques" (xiv).

# chapter 5

## Mental Illness/Chemical Dependence

### "Companion Demons"

[A father writes:] "Terry was dealt a doubly cruel hand: the companion demons depression and alcoholism. . . . After her teenage years the demons were always after her, relentlessly pulling at her stability and happiness. They took turns battering her with sadness and despair, which no doctor or medication seemed able to resolve. . . . Yet she persisted through countless AA meetings, numerous treatment facilities, hospitals, detox centers, and spiritual quests, and a thousand counseling sessions. . . . But in the end the demons won the physical battle and dragged her battered body to an untimely grave."
—George McGovern, *Terry*, xiii

Year after year after year. Hope does not spring eternal, but it may last a long time. There is a new medication, a highly recommended rehabilitation program, a therapist who really seems to care. But then the medication fails or the patient refuses to take it. The recovery doesn't last. The therapist is transferred. And the patient is back in the hospital, or detox center, or jail, or rooming house, or street. Meanwhile parents grow old, retire, die. Siblings graduate college, marry, divorce, start careers, change careers, travel, return. Children grow into adulthood and have children of their own. All of this happens in a world that those with severe mental illness or chemical dependence visit rarely, if at all.

They may not recognize family members for a while, then suddenly recognize them all too well—lashing out in terrifying rages. They are on their own interior journey, insensible to the havoc they are causing in the lives of those who love—or remember having loved—them. Mental illness and chemical dependence are frequent but not inevitable partners. They are linked here because they share a common trajectory.

The first indication that something is wrong often appears in adolescence or early adulthood. Parents and siblings usually recall an intelligent, loving child who is transformed overnight into an unrecognizable stranger. Of her brother's first breakdown Elizabeth Swados writes: "The easiest way to understand his schizophrenia was to believe it didn't exist. My parents, worn out from advice, deeply concerned about their reputation in the community, preferred to suffer from the notion that there was something wrong with their son, but that he could fix it himself with the best medical help, discipline, and determination" (*The Four of Us*, 29).

Because adolescents and young adults are often unpredictable and prone to experimenting with different life-styles, the first breakdown is rarely recognized as the beginning of a long journey. As time passes, the authors comb through the past for danger signs they might have missed, even as they find comfort in the warming experiences they find there. George McGovern remembers Terry as a fun-loving daughter at play with her brothers and sisters. Jay Neugeboren remembers Robert as the younger brother who shared his childhood bedroom and dreams.

Adult children cherish early memories of a caring parent. If the onset of mental illness or chemical dependence is delayed but a decade, a mother or father has time enough to imprint a positive image. Christopher Dickey remembers a father who taught him about nature and poetry. Jackie Lyden has pictures of herself in the costumes her mother created for her. Tara Holley, whose birth coincided with her mother's first breakdown, is one of the few authors who has no memories of her own—so she borrows those of her aunts. Their reminiscences of her mother as a young vocalist on the cusp of success achieve iconic status in the life of the family, symbolizing all that it has lost.

When it becomes clear that things are not going to get better on their own, authors embark on a search for aid. They have not yet exhausted their financial or emotional resources—which is fortunate, because the search is neither easy nor cheap. Private psychiatrists, hospitals, and rehab centers are the first port of call. With varying degrees of insight, the professionals suggest a course of treatment that promises hope for recovery. All that is asked of the patient and family is that they cooperate with the treatment plan laid out for them. Patients typically comply for a while; either they are in a setting that allows for no choice or they themselves believe in the possibility of cure. However, the constraints of treatment soon become clear—the disturbing side effects of medications, the therapy that seems to go nowhere, the call of a past life-style, a breakthrough of the illness—and they drop out.

Patients have begun their on-again, off-again relationship with the health care system. Their child, sibling, or parent may become unmoored but the family members hang on to the deck. At least for a while. They follow recommendations to different doctors, different approaches. They attend family groups. They learn a new language. Is the patient "a danger to herself or others?" Should they practice "unconditional acceptance" or "tough love"? They receive many opinions. At the time that Terry freezes to death on the snowbank onto which she has fallen in an alcoholic stupor, McGovern is following a counselor's advice that he be "less deeply involved" in her daily life. He never forgives himself.

Writing of her mother, Tara Holley sums up the problem: "I had tried everything I could think of to keep her off the street: temporary confinement in a hospital, halfway houses, motel rooms I paid for out of my own pocket. Nothing was ever settled: never could I tell myself, 'At last I've found the place' " (*In the Shadow of Schizophrenia*, 296).

As the years roll on, all but the very rich find they must turn to public agencies—state mental hospitals, public assistance, shelters—for help. Here they find a system of care that mirrors the chaotic and incomprehensible behavior of the patients.[1] Understaffing, undertraining, and lack of interest are endemic. Psychiatrists are seen as rushed drug dispensers whose rare forays into psychological interpretation do more harm than good. Common problems with medication—such as oversedation or disturbing side effects—are ignored or changes prescribed without explanation. Social workers, counselors, and nurses receive more credit. Many are seen as offering concrete help and practical advice. They are appreciated for taking the time to listen and to offer human connection and support. But sooner or later they disappoint; hindered by large caseloads and insufficient resources, they are unable to follow through on their treatment plans. Moreover, there is a rapid turnover in such jobs, and the memoir author wearies of repeating the long, sad history of a loved one to each new worker.

The patient's ability to understand what is going on is not static: it ebbs and flows with the course of the disease and the effectiveness of the current treatment. Professionals may disagree on what level of awareness constitutes "competence," forcing caregivers to make unilateral decisions with no clear guidelines. Accepting the best of bad alternatives comes hard. Any illness can cause distressing physical changes in the patient. But the cumulative assaults of self-neglect and injury on the lives of the mentally ill and addicted are particularly harrowing for the authors to witness. Elizabeth Swados's brother careers through life with an amputated right leg and arm—suffered when he threw himself in front of a subway train many years before. Unwashed, reeking of body odor, he is not alone among the patients in this section. Some are described as gaunt. Others are toothless. Seeing them in such a state, unable even to make them comfortable and clean, symbolizes the powerlessness of the author.

To this burden is added the unanswerable question of cause. Parents feel that they must be to blame. Siblings wonder how they escaped. Adult children feel at risk. Since no one can tell them why this fate has befallen them, families come to their own conclusions. Society provides a ready-made list of reasons. What family tree does not have an alcoholic, mentally ill, or somewhat peculiar member somewhere in its branches? How many people reach adulthood without losing at least one beloved person to distance, divorce, or death? Who has grown up in a family devoid of conflict?

George McGovern turns up alcoholic relatives on his side of the family, his wife's postpartum depression after Terry's birth, and his own time away on the political trail while she was growing up. Remembering an early family life colored by his parents' unhappy marriage, Jay Neugeboren decides that his brother identified with the weaknesses of their parents while he identified with their strengths. Elizabeth Swados and Margaret Moorman do not seek reasons; they simply accept that that they must present a happy and "normal" face to the world—and so vindicate their parents' embarrassment over having a damaged child.

Adult children greet each year that passes with relief—the longer they live without developing symptoms of their parent's illness, the safer they feel. A few, like Tara Holley, seek the counsel of psychiatrists in reckoning the odds. More often, they act out their fears by life choices, recognizing the meanings of their actions only in retrospect. Christopher Dickey battens himself down: he marries and has a child while barely out of his teens. Jackie Lyden loosens her ties: she jumps on horseback and tours with a rodeo. By such decisive acts they claim control over their own lives, separating themselves from parents who are blatantly out of control.

The stories written by those who cared for the mentally ill or chemically dependent bear a stylistic resemblance. Less chronological, more circular, than memoirs of other illnesses, they reflect the need to reconcile healthy and sick images of their family member, to recapture all the positive moments and commemorate periods of normality. No matter how few they are in number, good memories prove crucial in sustaining the authors through the long decades that follow.

There is likely to be a changing cast of involved family members. Some drop out once and for all. Others come and go. Authors are often the only ones left to bear witness to the entire story. Eight years after her son's diagnosis, Swados's mother died of an overdose of sleeping pills. Neugeboren's mother, an active participant in her son's treatment for eight years—going so far as to run mental health fundraising events—decides, at the age of sixty-two, to move to Florida. " 'I've done all I can do,' she said. 'Let the state take over. You be in charge from now on, Jay—I just can't handle it anymore' " (*Imagining Robert*, 20).

A few trips through the revolving door of the system and the meanings attached to the illness change. The mentally ill patient will not return to being the person once known. The chemically dependent patient will probably relapse. The health and social welfare system does not hold the magic key. The authors then begin the struggle to find a degree of separation that will allow them to live their own lives without abandoning their loved ones. An on-again, off-again pattern of involvement now emerges, reflecting the lifelong nature of the disease, the fact that the patient often rejects care, and a growing realization that no one person can be expected to shoulder all the burden. Sometimes it is the patient who pushes them away. Sometimes the authors, in the interests of their own mental health, find they must remove themselves from the scene. Yet it is always understood that one day the call that cannot be ignored will come. And they will return.

For those caregivers who cannot leave, the separation becomes internal. Like Tara Holley, whose mother is the homeless woman she passes each day on her way to college classes, they remain physically involved but their beliefs change. They begin to accept a situation that once would have been unthinkable. They stop looking to professionals for the answer. Now they look to the patient and to themselves.

As hopes for large changes fade, appreciation of small changes grows. Where caregivers once saw only failure, they now see a valiant struggle for survival. Tara Holley's mother sells flowers to motorists stopped at a traffic light. Elizabeth Swados's brother plays a harmonica, a cup for contributions at his feet. George McGovern's daughter sustains one eight-year period of sobriety in twenty-five years of adulthood. Jackie Lyden's mother uses her manic creativeness to start a mail order business. Aware of the difficulty that their loved ones have simply getting through each day, the authors view these efforts as triumphs.

By finding islands of normality in a sea of craziness, refusing to let the individuality of their loved ones be swept away in a tide of symptoms, many authors of the mental illness/chemical dependence experience sustain themselves through the years they are called upon to care.

There are two endings to the journey. A horrible death is, sadly, still common. The ambiguous character of many of these deaths—not intentional suicides but clear consequences of chemical dependence or mental illness—are particularly difficult to bear. The freezing death of McGovern's daughter is matched by the ending of Swados's brother—his body is found locked up in a windowless shed erected in front of the abandoned storefront he had been occupying. Greg Bottom's brother is serving a long sentence in a prison ward for the criminally insane. Other patients die slowly and painfully as a consequence of their disease; both of Dickey's parents die of alcohol-related causes. And Ann Patchett's friend Lucy Grealy dies of an overdose that did not seem to be planned. The fact that these deaths often occur at a time when the authors have temporarily suspended involvement with their loved ones is an everlasting source of regret.

Others are alive and doing better at the memoir's end: a tribute to new classes of medication that had come into widespread use by the 1990s. Jackie Lyden's mother is stabilized on Lithium. Tara Holley's mother does well on Chlorazil. They do not emerge from years of illness as whole and happy people able to make up for lost time. The wear and tear of their difficult lives has taken its toll on body and spirit. Advancing age and the side effects of the drugs do the rest. They are subdued shadows of who they could have been. Medication alone is not enough; therapy and a lot of concrete and emotional support from family is needed to sustain improvement. So much time has passed. So many helpers present at the beginning are no longer available. Still, the remaining family members soldier on. And for some, the right drug is still to be found. After a promising beginning on Risperidone, Jay Neugeboren's brother suffers a relapse. His hopes dashed once again, he responds, "I feel, simply, very sad, and enormously tired" (299).

Next to stories of lives that ended or improved at midlife after decades of struggle are a cluster of memoirs by parents describing the events leading up to the suicides of their children. Memoirs by parents whose children died by their own hand bear striking resemblances. For the most part, they are written by widely recognized public figures. Danielle Steele is a best-selling author of romance fiction, and Gloria Vanderbilt is internationally recognized as an heiress and fashion designer. Substance use and mental illness come together in most of these situations. Like McGovern's daughter, who was brought down by alcohol, Steele's son dies of an overdose of narcotics. Even though their children had problems with substances before, these endings are seen as ambiguous. It is hard to believe that they really meant to take their lives. Gloria Vanderbilt's son jumps off the terrace of their apartment. She does not accept that it was a suicide, believing instead that his action was caused by a prescription drug that brought on a sleepwalking dream. As all the other lost children, he had so much to live for. Prominent psychiatrists and private hospitals, loving families and paid attendants did not, in the end, make a difference. Celebrity authors consciously use their name recognition to raise public awareness and, with the profits from their books, establish foundations to research the causes and cure of such untimely deaths.

Whatever the outcome of the long journey, all the authors would agree with Martha Tod Dudman as she reflects on her experience finding help for her troubled adolescent daughter: "We were all just thrashing through the woods in darkness. There was no map" (*Augusta Gone*, 252).

# part 2
## Care Relationships

Love gives us the right to hold contradictory judgments about ourselves, about the ones we love; we discover truths that would be in absurd opposition if they hadn't been spun in love's loom.
—C. K. Williams

# chapter 6
## Introduction
### "Spun in Love's Loom"

Portraying the fragile, complex, and ever-changing nature of the author's family bonds is the raison d'être of most memoirs. Authors sort out the contradictions of love, untwist the strands to their beginnings, and weave them anew. A tapestry of meaning, adding breadth and depth to the caring experience.

Who *is* the person, now the patient, and why should we share the author's concern for his life and his memory? And what can be told of the relationship before this point that will make its importance clear to us? Like novelists and playwrights, memoirists must find an opportune place and method of inserting the "back story." Unlike novelists and playwrights, they cannot insert illuminating references to the past in the conversations of fictional characters or present them in the voice of an omnipotent narrator.

Photographs are a stylistic shortcut. At once the most transparent and enigmatic of devices authors employ, photographs are commonly used as adjuncts to the text. The number of photographs, their placement within the book (spaced throughout or confined to the centerfold), the presence or absence of explanatory captions, and the wording of captions that do appear form a counternarrative that sometimes illustrates, sometimes contradicts the authors' words.

Collectively fit for Kodak advertisements of generic family life in the last half of the twentieth century, most photographs in memoirs feature classic scenes: vacations at mountain or shore, the wedding party in full dress, newborns in the arms of beaming parents and grandparents, everyone gathered around the birthday cake or Christmas tree. Scenes of family happiness, capturing a long-gone moment. Such photographs—along with studio-posed sepia prints of earlier generations—carry a particular poignancy for the reader, who is viewing them in the light of the knowledge of all that followed.

In an in-depth analysis of the use of photography in autobiography, Adams (2000) suggests that captioned photos are a way for authors to maintain control, that their explanations rob readers of the opportunity to take their own cues. His notion does not hold up in regard to memoirs of family care: to the contrary, captions are at times so at odds with the text as to leave readers wondering if they say more about the relationship than the author intended. Take, for example, the captions that Andrew Malcolm chooses for the photographs of his mother through the various stages of her life: "New mother and her son," "Wife of a retired man," "A widow." The passage of time is writ clear on her face and form. In the first she is bursting with vitality, in the last feeble and near death. The reader can't help but observe that the captions portray her in a series of roles in relation to the men in her life. And ask: Would she have seen herself that way? Could some of the late-life behavior that her son characterized as vain and foolish have been, in fact, a need to claim an existence in her own right? More consistent with the message of the text is Clara Claiborne Park's caption of a photograph of her autistic daughter: "With characteristic concentration, Jessy checks the accuracy of her painting against a photographed detail." The scientific detachment that belies the fact that this is a mother speaking of her child typifies the approach that Park took to documenting her findings and so enhancing professional knowledge about autism.

Then there are the ubiquitous author photographs, sometimes featuring author and the family member cared for in the same shot. So it is that the reader stops short at the photograph of Jay Neugeboren side by side with the mentally ill brother he has watched over for decades. They share a strong family resemblance and a troubled expression, leading the viewer to ask: Who is the patient here? Such ironies, intended or accidental, abound in juxtapositions of text and photographs—tangible reflections of the contradictions of love.

When it comes to inserting the "back story," dreams and reveries are as frequently invoked as photographs. Reveries are often used as segues from an incident in the present to its antecedent in the past, as when Annie Ernaux's slow gentle brushing of her mother's hair recalls a time when she was a child and her mother harshly and hurriedly performed the same actions for her. Some dreams are presented in small comprehensible fragments while others are as convoluted and nonsensical as dreams usually are. In memoirs, as in life, the dreamers are sole interpreters of their dream, tailoring the telling in accordance with their analysis of how it fits in with their nondream lives. Dead parents or their younger selves return in dreams to offer counsel. Authors enter into other dimensions of time and space, where their worldly thoughts and actions acquire new perspective.

As compelling as photographs, dreams, and reveries are in conveying the back story of the family care experience, they are more than matched by the power of anecdote. Tales that have been told many times, they carry the patina of long use; rough patches and edges smoothed, a clearly demarcated beginning, middle, and end—as polished and set apart as a gem among the flotsam and jetsam of daily life. Anecdotes are characterized by a common cast of characters and story line. Featuring authors and/or family members whose care is the centerpiece of the memoir, they ostensibly tell of an incident in their past lives while subtly showcasing their personalities and relationships before the health crisis.

Depicting deeply fractured or ambivalent relationships (most common in memoirs of sibling and parent care) are anecdotes spaced throughout the text that illustrate both positive and negative views of the ill or disabled family member. More than a few of these conflicted authors also portray their earlier selves in an unflattering light. Guilty of sins of omission—most often, being unappreciative of what they had when they had it—they seek redemption through caring. In memoirs of child care and spouse/life-partner care, anecdotes are more often elegiac: depicting authors and subjects in a remembered

Eden—their best moments as individuals and as a family memorialized and offered as counterpoint to their worst.

The photographs, anecdotes, and reveries on which the patient's identity is constructed are chosen and shaped by the author. But why these and not others? What, indeed, gives authors the right to write one side of a story—a story that, moreover, is based on the illness or disability of someone other than themselves? Would the philosopher/novelist Iris Murdoch wish to be remembered for her writing or for her last days as an Alzheimer's patient so reduced in intellect that she is unable to care for her own basic needs? Her husband's memoir—like the memoirs of Anne Morrow Lindbergh's daughter and James Dickey's son—portray the darkest, most diminished hours of individuals previously known only for their accomplishments. Then there are well-known authors—like Simone de Beauvoir, Danielle Steele, Jamaica Kincaid, Philip Roth—who write of family members of whom the reader has never before heard. None lived to read the portrayal of them in the memoir's pages. What would they have said? The reader will never know.

Struggles with the ethics of "appropriation" that invariably arise in professional discussions of illness narratives are remarkably absent from memoirs of family care. Most authors are clear: the story reflects their point of view and is theirs to tell as they see fit. A few authors make a point of including the words or artwork of other family members, or the relatives on whom the narrative is based, tacitly acknowledging other perspectives on the story. The motives of the author—personal as well as stylistic—contribute to the sidelining or exclusion of other actors. Amid a wash of family recollection, there are many people who must have been involved at key scenes who are mentioned glancingly if at all. Yet even in their absence, these figures cast a long shadow. *Their* stories would probably have been different—in what ways, the reader can only imagine.

Whatever their ages or family roles (indeed whatever the illnesses or disabilities), authors describe family care as a continuous process of risk assessment. From a father deciding whether to place his marginally retarded child in a special education class to a wife deciding whether to take a vacation trip with a partner with severe heart disease, to a sister authorizing an operation that would sterilize her mentally disabled sister, to an adult child deciding whether a mother with Alzheimer's Disease can safely live alone, balancing risk against reward is a recurring theme.

When life-altering decisions for ill or disabled relatives are involved, the author must frequently choose the lesser of two evils—a choice that is doubly hard when the family member whose life will be most affected is incapable or unwilling to participate. One decision invariably leads to another. Options narrow. Outside pressures and lack of sufficient information about alternatives plague the authors. Yet they soldier on in the face of uncertainty and constraints.

Memoirs provide the opportunity for hindsight. Retrospectively reviewing the outcome of their decisions as well as detailing the process leading up to them, authors spare no one, least of all themselves. Indeed, choices serve as pivotal points in the memoirs. They mark transitions—not only in the treatment and life-style conditions of ill or disabled family members but in the ways that authors think and feel about them.

What possesses one family member to drop everything to be by the side of an ailing relative while another stays away until the last possible moment? There is a cultural expectation that parents will take care of their minor children and that spouses and life partners will stick together "in sickness and in health." But what of relationships where the expectations are more ambiguous and the feelings more ambivalent?

Memoirs of sibling and parent care show that there is no easy formula. Sisters may be estranged, fathers may have been alcoholic or neglectful, mothers may have thwarted their early attempts at independence, causing them to flee. Yet their siblings and their children return to care. Duty, compassion, a desire to get the love or recognition that they didn't before—these are only a few of their complicated motivations. These authors care because it is impossible for them not to care. And through the process of giving more than they feel they have ever received, they are sometimes able to forge a more satisfying relationship before the end. Even when they are not successful in making things better, they have the satisfaction of knowing that their conflicted and often angry feelings did not prevent them from doing the "right thing."

Caregiving is a reciprocal relationship. Although cognitively impaired children or parents may be unable to recognize or "give back," it doesn't matter. As different as their care situations may be, authors speak with one voice on what they have learned about life and about love through such caring. It is in memoirs of age cohorts (siblings, spouses, and life partners), however, that the theme of mutuality is best delineated. Whatever way these peers are joined, they share a generational bond sufficiently elastic to allow reciprocity throughout the care process.

The few memoirs written about the care of unrelated others are particularly enlightening. What propelled the authors (admittedly few in number) to write a memoir about the care of friends? Relationship characteristics are constant across memoirs. Primary are the facts that the recipients of care had weak or nonexistent family ties (free space around them, which provided a point of entry) and had some personality qualities with which the author identified. Understanding their friends—through writing about their encounters with illness and disability—thus became an exercise in self-discovery.

"Outsider" status—real or perceived, past or present—cements these caring connections. Because Abraham Verghese and his friend David are both newcomers to the community and both in the throes of troubled personal relationships, their time together playing tennis is infused with meaning beyond the shared activity. The same may be said for the very different situation of Calving Trillin and his college friend Denny, whose status as middle-class graduates of public high schools marked them as "other" in the upper-class, post–prep school environment of Yale in the 1950s. Or of Ann Patchett and Lucy Grealy, whose sexual inexperience and literary aspirations marked them as different from their peers. Teresa McGee and her friend Jim are devout Catholics who have each faced a crisis of faith. Amy Hoffman and her friend Michael are part of the gay community at the worst moments of the AIDS epidemic. A connection at a deep level of their beings ties the fate of one friend to another friend, even as the world might wonder why.

In an introduction to Hoffman's memoir, Urvashi Vaid notes, "This book points out the tremendous expansion of the idea of traditional family that lesbian and gay people have effected, an expansion that

AIDS further cemented. . . . How did a people so ostracized by an institution end up reinventing it?" (*Hospital Time*, ix–x). What does it mean for a collection of friends and colleagues to act as family? In these ambiguously structured situations, how much can one expect from others? From oneself? Most provocative in these stories of friend care is the reconstruction of the human qualities thought of as being inextricable from "family values" or family caregiving.

The chapters that follow are organized according to role relationships between authors and their subjects. Grandparents are included in the discussion of child care. Life partners join spouses in the discussion of couple care. Each relationship is represented by memoirs that depict the care experience from a range of ages, life stages, and family structures. Parents are young or mid-life. Partners may be newlyweds or have passed a golden anniversary. Adult children may have felt born to care from their earliest years, or be seniors themselves before they hear the call. All individual stories, yet they share a palette of actions, thoughts, and feelings out of which meanings are created.

# chapter 7
## Child Care
### "An Unimagined Life"

> [A mother writes:] "This experience we did not choose, which we would have given anything to avoid, has made us different, has made us better. Through it we have learned the lesson that no one studies willingly, the hard, slow lesson of Sophocles and Shakespeare—that one grows by suffering. And that too is Jessy's gift. . . . Out of it has come, for all of us, an unimagined life."
> —Clara Claiborne Park, *The First Eight Years*, 320

A son is born with a growth on his brain so large that it looks as if he has two heads. An eleven-year-old daughter is hit by a car and paralyzed from the neck down. A six-year-old son comes down with what had seemed like an ordinary flu, leukemia is diagnosed, and he dies within months while doctors stand helplessly by. A brilliant teenager succumbs to addiction and suicide.

The world is not supposed to work like this. Boys and girls are supposed to grow into self-sufficient men and women, to move from dependence to independence; and in time, to care for their frail parents. For a mother or father, the severe disability or fatal illness of a child is an earthquake: the very ground on which their lives have been constructed has shifted—and they struggle to find footing in an altered universe. As Heather Choate Davis, whose baby daughter was diagnosed with cancer, writes: "There was no more lightness in the world, no grace, no logic, no hope, no master plan. No one was watching over us, goodness was not rewarded, and darkness was all around" (*Baptism by Fire*, 32).

The memoir authors watch as all around them unscathed families celebrate their children's developmental milestones in a world where tricycles inevitably lead to bicycles, and each grade of school prepares for the next. The sting of being singled out for tragedy came at a time of life when the authors were least prepared for it. Most were under the age of forty, still settling into the responsibilities of adult life—balancing demands of family and work, worried over financial and job insecurities, finding an acceptable degree of separation from their own parents.

Now they are faced with the harshest of truths. The fatally ill child will suffer unto death. The developmentally delayed child or autistic child will face a future of stigma and limited life choices. The child who has fallen prey to accident or addiction will not fulfill his early potential.

The first question is always "why." Causes are forthcoming: an extra chromosome, a careless driver, a chemical imbalance, a runaway cancer cell. Reasons are harder to come by. And it is a reason—an explanation for the inexplicable—that distraught parents seek. Seeking someone or something to blame is a common, if short-lived, response. Even in the case of accidents when a careless driver was plainly culpable, the authors realize early on that they can't dissipate their energies in anger. (Laura Kramer, who believes her son's cerebral palsy to be the direct result of a botched delivery, sued the obstetrician, recovering sufficient money to pay for his special needs. But her situation is the exception to the rule.)

Abandonment of the search for a reason marks a turning point. It occurs at different points for different authors, but the time always arrives. They come to believe that there is only one possible version of the story: the child that was born to them is the only child that could have been. The question is no longer "why" but "how."

Like earthquake survivors searching in the rubble for pieces of a former life to salvage, cobble together, and use in new ways, the authors call upon the people and ideas that have helped them in the past. Whether these disappointed or surpassed expectations (and there are many examples of both), they eventually take hold of the new situation and deal with it as best they can.

The authors want it known that they are not stoics, saints, or seers. They felt their children's physical and psychic suffering in their own bones. They wondered if they had the skill or the stamina to do all that needed doing—and how long it would go on. They were exhausted. They were despondent. They wished to be done with it. Kenzaburo Oë recalls his initial reluctance to approve lifesaving surgery for a son who would remain severely disabled even after the operation. When Louise Ray Morningstar first heard that her daughter was critically injured in an automobile accident, she wished for death rather than suffering. J. T. McDonnell was shocked to hear a mother in her support group confess to a feeling of "relief" at the death of an emotionally disturbed son—then flirted briefly with the idea herself. And yet, they keep walking toward the light—groping about in the shadows, searching for familiar shapes to orient them.

Reverend Jimmy Allen and Rabbi Harold Kushner look to Biblical teachings and commentary. For lay people like Heather Choate Davis, Louise Ray Morningstar, and Gordon Livingston, the response of a community of faith is a great solace. Prayer circles, pastoral visits paid to home and hospital, linkages to other congregations when medical treatment pulled child and parent far from home—all are noted with profound gratitude.

Others return to secular sources of meaning. Oë compares his personal catastrophe with that of his country. Hiroshima became the touchstone to which he returned—hoping to find in the words of those who survived their horror words to help him in his. Professionals and academics look to the areas of study in which they have invested their educational lives. Steeped in post-modern literary theory, Michael Berube is more than prepared to challenge a conception of "normality" that would place his son with Down's Syndrome on the wrong side of a great divide. Investigating the tyranny of testing standards—and their limitations in measuring the uniqueness of each child—becomes a research interest. The philosophical implications of mathematics and physics—what is necessary, what is contingent—help Joan L. Richards make decisions about her son's care.

The authors do not wish themselves or their children to become objects of pity. They struggle to define the situation on their own terms—to create and maintain an ordinary life in an extraordinary situation. And yet the dying or disabled child exerts a centrifugal force, influencing every area of their lives. There are the hospital stays where one parent puts in 24/7 time, often for weeks on end. There are special schools—often at some distance—which the child has to be delivered to and picked up from. There are hours of remedial or rehabilitation exercises. Family, friends, neighbors, and paid helpers come and go. Not a moment is free of reminders that theirs is not a typical family.

Worries over the development of well siblings, questions over the risk of bearing additional children, who may inherit the same problem or not receive their fair share of attention, job pressures, and financial insecurity—all bedevil these parents. Unprepared for so many challenges, the authors maintain an uneasy equilibrium even as they try to keep their lives as normal as possible.

Some authors glide over the marital fallout surrounding an ill child. While they allude to the facts—the reconfigured division of labor as one parent kept the home fires burning while the other did hospital duty, the agreements and disagreements in making care plans, the difficulty of coordinating everyone's schedules—they tread lightly on the emotions arising from them. A few let the reader in to reveal a tightrope relationship in which anger over the burden of care can become projected onto the spouse.

Younger as well as older siblings share the care—helpful and caring, rejoicing in the ill or disabled child's accomplishments, grieving over setbacks, an extra pair of hands in accomplishing family tasks. A few act out in undesirable ways, but the majority try to excel at every developmental milestone—to make up for the child who can't. As the authors watch all of this happen they are alternately flooded with gratitude and with fear. When does being good become being too good? When Kramer observed that her son had become dependent on his younger sister to tie his shoes before school each morning, she made a point of taking over the job herself. The act took only a few minutes from her daughter's life; yet freeing her from the responsibility was recognition that her needs were as important as his.

As their ill or disabled children long to join in the activities of unimpaired peers, the authors consider the risks and rewards of letting them try. As a limitless future could not be the destiny of their dying children, they learn how to cram as much living as possible into the finite now. Like Mary-Lou Weisman, they decide that their children's lives have to be about "quality—about how well, how deep, how rich—not about how fast, how many, how soon, how long" (*Intensive Care*, 65).

Authors are fierce in the search for aid for their children. After observing how others parents found their ways around the system, the authors struck out on their own. They learned new skills: therapeutic techniques to practice at home, sign language to communicate better with a Down's Syndrome son, how to give injections and change medical dressings. A host of skilled nursing tasks that they initially felt ill equipped for soon become second nature.

When surgery or medication is the recommended treatment, the authors remain deferential to medical authority. When it is not, they question professional advice. Confident that they know themselves and their children better than any outsider could, they accept what makes sense and ignore the rest. Often they combine information from a variety of sources: tailoring an assessment and treatment to meet their individual needs. As time passes, they care less about how professionals view them—and are prepared to be seen as pushy or pestering if it brings about the desired result. When rules do not take their children's well-being into account, they see no reason to follow them. In order to ease the irritation of loosened braces, Louise Ray Morningstar smuggled a forbidden dentist into her comatose daughter's hospital room. To spare her chemotherapy-bald son the embarrassment of looking strange, Marlys Lehman mounted a winning battle to challenge the "no hats" policy at his school. Both mothers amazed themselves with their actions. Nothing in their lives had prepared them for subversion or confrontation, but in the service of their children they were fearless.

Many of the authors were trailblazers. The strategy that Clara Claiborne Park devised for breaking through the isolation of her autistic daughter later served as a professional model. Michael Dorris identified fetal alcohol syndrome in his adopted son and raised society's awareness of its prevalence and devastation. Some authors were among the first to benefit from newly emerging treatments. For Kenzaburo Oë, this was lifesaving surgery on his newborn son. Jane Bernstein and Martha Moraghan Jablow found themselves and their baby daughters in "infant stim" classes. Here they observed compassionate and skillful staff, children who looked like their own, mothers who shared their struggles. They learned that they were not alone.[1]

Many authors use the metaphor of war. Park titled the first of her three books about her autistic daughter, Jessy, "The Siege"—aptly portraying her efforts to break through her daughter's isolation. Referring to the bedside vigil of his dying son, Gordon Livingston wrote: "This situation resembles combat in that it really can't be explained in all its horror, exhaustion, and anxiety to someone who hasn't experienced it" (*Only Spring*, 49).

As in a war, the landscape of the authors is perpetually in flux and strategic decisions are made on the basis of limited knowledge. Would the child survive to adulthood? If so, with how much ability to function on his own? Would the child die of his illness or injuries? If so, how best could his remaining days on earth be spent? Questions that are hard for the authors to ask are often impossible for professionals to answer. So the authors make choices day by day in an atmosphere of ambiguity. There is also the presence of a constantly ticking clock. For once their ill or disabled children become old enough to make decisions for themselves, the authors have to reconsider the degree of their involvement.

All wish to see their ill or disabled child go to school and have friends, and all rejoice in individual milestones (celebrating birthdays, riding a bike, attending a ballgame, spending a night away from home, occupying a valued role in the life of the family). In short, they want their children to participate in the larger world to the full extent of their capacities. This poses another problem. As Jane McDonnell, the mother of an autistic son, wrote: "If I pushed him too hard to be like other children his age, wouldn't I simply be teaching him the deeper lesson that he was flawed?" (*Notes from the Border*, 266).

For the developmentally disabled child, the author's choice was often to find a new peer group with whom he could identify—a group where performance expectations were lower and others shared his problems. This was rarely an option when the child's difficulty was not visible or pervasive. McDonnell and Kramer have sons who wrote well enough to contribute chapters to their mother's books. But both were teenagers with a difference. Paul McDonnell was subject to disorientation and rages. Seth Kramer had trouble tying his shoes and walked with a lopsided gait. Able in some areas, not in others—they and their parents moved between the world of the "normal" and the world of the "disabled," feeling ill at ease in both.

The choices are fewer—and in some ways easier—when the child's disabilities were obvious from birth; then the major challenge becomes finding that special classroom or special school where their child is accepted for who he is. Such a setting is rarely found at the first try. Finances, distance, and family scheduling all have to be negotiated. Through it all, the authors refuse to see their child as one of a class, one of "them." Like Berube, who lovingly describes the ways of his Down's Syndrome's son as "sui generis"—they discover that beneath a shared genetic legacy their disabled children are all individuals.

When an accident befalls a normally developing child, the authors are suddenly plunged into an all-consuming involvement reminiscent of the first months of that child's life. One period of uncertainty follows another. Would they survive at all? To what extent would they regain physical and intellectual functioning? Would they be able to pick up their life's trajectory where they left off? It takes months, sometimes years, of waiting and watching for the answers to come—a period of time when the authors step out of their own lives to become full-time attendants to their children. They take leaves of absence from jobs, from spouses, from their other children. They leave their homes behind, moving into hospitals and rehabilitation centers. In their round-the-clock attendance at the bedside, aware of the slightest shifts of posture or facial expression, the outside world recedes from their view. Often their child's recovery is marked by personality changes. For some authors it is like accepting a changeling— in many ways still the son or daughter that they knew, and in many ways different. The memoirs of Karen Brennan and Louise Ray Morningstar are particularly effective in portraying this situation.

Authors speak with one voice when it comes to rejecting pity over their atypical lives and emphasizing the ways in which their families are like all others. As Mary-Lou Weisman wrote: "While Peter was dying, he was living. . . . He was an entire person, . . . who went to school, rode a bike, talked dirty and got into trouble. . . . And those of us who cared for him were whole people too, . . . who went to work, had friends, made love and paid bills. We were not just tragic figures" (*Intensive* Care, x).

It is not always easy to maintain such normality. Even when the prognosis is grim, physicians—often parents themselves who can identify with the prospect of losing a child—suggest experimental treatments. Some authors who acted aggressively are comforted by knowing they tried everything. Like Doris Lund and Donna Breen they learn to cherish times of remission by helping their children live them to the fullest and accept inevitable hospitalizations and setbacks as the price to be paid. But Gordon Livingston, himself a physician, has cause for regret. Going along with the bone marrow transplant recommended turned out to increase the suffering of his six-year-old son without prolonging his life. Grief at the death is compounded by anger with himself at making the choice. Authors who chose not to follow medical advice faced the disapproval of their doctors as well as their own inner doubts. Yet some took the chance. Weighing an unpredictable outcome against a knowable present, Weisman decided against a recommended surgery that would incapacitate her still-active son.

The wisdom of the adage "it takes a village to raise a child" is never more applicable than when that child is seriously ill or disabled. The nuclear family is not sufficient to handle such an assault. Memoir after memoir attests the importance of committed others. Theirs is a world more heavily populated than that of any other authors. Grandparents, aunts, uncles, friends, neighbors, parishioners, co-workers, students, bosses march across their pages. They offer more than shoulders to cry on, such as practical help (with the house, with the other children, with work adjustments); they fly in for visits; some decide to move in for awhile. Some are credited with major contributions of time and skill. Others might have pitched in only once. Together they make it possible for the authors to get through each day. Awareness that one need not handle every burden of life alone, that there are good people who can lend a hand, is a revelation to some of these young parents, whose academic and work lives have been geared toward competition and independence.

Survivors of the earthquake, battle-scarred veterans of many campaigns, authors who cared for disabled children have seen their worst fears come true. Meeting each challenge as it arose, they grew stronger as they went along. Although their grief was heavy, it was tempered by the knowledge that they did what had to be done. In many memoirs the disabled child has grown up to take his place in the world—his well-being and whereabouts no longer controlled or controllable by loving family. Authors who had invested so much of their lives in caring for their children now have to be satisfied with caring about them. They learn to let go. Their children might continue to live with them. They might continue in a protected work or school environment. But they have developed into adults with adult sexual drives, adult desires for travel and adventure. As parents of well children adapt their parenting styles over the years, so do the authors who have children with disabilities.

Doing all they can to minimize risk, they learn to trust in the kindness of strangers. When her son Paul takes a trip, McDonnell tells him that if he becomes lost or confused he should look for a person who looks official—seated behind a desk, wearing a uniform—and present him with the letter that she has put in his backpack. The "To Whom It May Concern" letter explains his problem, has the address of the place he is headed for, and requests assistance in helping him reach it. "And then we sent him off into the wild blue yonder, the ether, . . . the lap of the gods" (*Notes from the Border*, 321–322).

The pain of having a different child never leaves, but the love for that child makes it bearable. Jane Bernstein writes of her daughter: "She will never be valued by the world. It would be a lie to say that I do not care. If there were a magic pill that would rid her of all deficits, I would give it to her, but I don't love her less for her imperfections; nor do I love her in spite of them. . . . I am with you, Rachel. I have learned to introduce you to the world and to be proud of you in the face of pity and ridicule" (*Loving Rachel*, 178, 279).

When a child dies the last thing parents want is "closure." Their greatest fear is of the slow attrition of memory. What he sounded like—his words, his voice—fades in time, loss within loss. They struggle to keep the ideas of their sons and daughters alive. They write about them: "His death, like that of any child, is a story of withered hopes and unfulfilled dreams. In this book I have tried to capture a few remembered strains of the brief, glad music of his life. These are all I have of him now, and they comfort me even as they break my heart" (*Only Spring*, xxi).

They set up memorials. Livingston raises funds for long-term rental of a hotel suite designated for the use of families of children being treated in an adjacent hospital. McGovern and Steele set up foundations for research into the causes and treatments of the conditions that claimed the lives of their children. And they go on living. As Rabbi Kushner advises, "Live their years along with your own, and feel their presence as you do so" (*When Bad Things Happen*, xiii).

# chapter 8

## Sibling Care

### "She Was My Parents' Child, And So Was I"

> She was my parents' child, and so was I. We were in this together, and I must have subconsciously thought as much. Otherwise, I would never have felt so much sorrow on her behalf, or so much fear of turning out to be like her.
>
> —Margaret Moorman, *My Sister's Keeper*, 77

They started out together—sharing a gene pool, a mother and a father, a childhood home. It may not have been foreseen. It surely wasn't fair. But one was destined to a damaged or foreshortened future, and the other to a better life. The story of sibling care is one of chained destinies—written by authors who are bound by identification with ill or disabled brothers and sisters even as they claim their right to a different path.

The story of sibling care usually spans years if not decades. It is rarely continuous, or "hands on." The most common pattern is intermittent periods of intense involvement alternating with longer periods of physical and emotional separation. Two paths emerge: that of the authors whose sibling's problems date from their shared time together in the childhood home and that of authors who drifted apart in adult life and came together at a point of crisis. Although these two paths often end up in the same place, the journeys are quite different.

As in memoirs of parent care, the present story is punctuated with encapsulated stories of a shared past, many dating back to the author's earliest memories. The number of children in the family, the siblings' birth position within it, the relationships between and among them, glimpses of mother and father as young parents, the tenor of that first home—all imbued with an adult understanding of where it all was leading .

Another similarity is the prominent role of regret: over relationships that never blossomed, over lost opportunities for reconciliation. Authors search for turning points—the moments that could have changed everything, if they knew then what they know now. But they too were young! Anger at what they went through mingles with the guilt of knowing that their siblings suffered far more. Back and forth they go, making a case for and against their actions and attitudes so many years ago.

The marked difference between memoirs of parent care and of sibling care is in the way authors deal with the recalled past and move on. Adult sons and daughters (as noted in that chapter) look to that past for their future. They are involved in an effort to seek and claim their legacy—what of the parents lives on in them. Brothers and sisters don't look to the past to see what of their siblings lives on in them—they look for reasons why they are different. Their need is not to rejoin but to separate—to trace the path from there to here and give themselves the right to a different ending.

Elizabeth Swados, whose brother had schizophrenia, writes of her teenage years: "I began the fantasy that I was living for the two of us, making up for the two of us, vindicating my parents as parents" (*The Four of Us*, 36). Those who grow up with impaired siblings are forever marked by the experience. They are model children whose competence is forever contrasted with that of brothers and sisters who lag behind. The inevitable attempt to reassure mothers and fathers that they are okay just as inevitably morphs into the attempt to reassure themselves. They pile up one achievement after another—struggling to escape the contagion of their siblings' conditions even as they meet the world laden with mingled feelings of pity and guilt.

The strain of being the child no one has to worry about occasionally becomes too much, and these model siblings may act out in a way that places them in the unaccustomed family spotlight—especially in adolescence, when sexual and drug experimentation is common. They may return to being the "good" sons and daughters, the ones who eventually end up on a productive life path. Still, the impulse to follow their siblings into a netherworld is strong. Maria Flook, who was twelve when her fourteen-year-old sister ran away from home, wrote, "I imagined that my every reckless act from that moment on was a stepping-stone to our reunion" (*My Sister Life*, 189).

With a home life so unlike those of their friends, their childhood is infused with a sense of being apart from the rest of the peers that echoes through a lifetime. Growing up between two worlds, with a foot in each, they have the sense expressed by Rachel Simon: "I would have to convey information from one to the other, never quite belonging to either" (*Riding the Bus with My Sister*, 10).

Adding to the author's sense of difference is silence about the ill sibling. Memoir after memoir recalls a childhood where the most obvious fact of life was rarely discussed. Outside of the home, it might have been stigma or a case of strangers not knowing quite what to say. Inside the home, there is a sense of secrecy, but also one of exhaustion. "We never talked about Michael, partly because his insane behavior was 'normal' to us, partly because it was too much to deal with to put our feelings into words and exchange them" (Greg Bottoms, *Angelhead*, 59).

Authors who grew up with ill or disabled siblings enter adulthood with a sense of encumbrance. It does not prevent them from moving out and moving on. They go off to school, to careers, and to relationships as they were meant to do. But it is always with a sense of discomfort: at the good fortune a brother or a sister cannot share, at the knowledge that responsibility for that sibling's well-being will one day be in their hands.

When the day inevitably arrives, it presents a problem unique to the sibling relationship. How much are siblings expected to do for one another? How are they ever to know if they are doing the right thing? Society endorses the responsibility of parents for dependent children and adult children for aging parents, but is unclear on the subject of siblings.

When Bob Smith was just coming of age, his parents placed his beloved retarded sister, Caroline, in an institution. Decades passed before he could bring himself to visit. Should he have undone a decision that he had no share in making?[1] Physical separation of such magnitude is rare. More often, the ill or disabled sibling remains in the community and the author acts as an alter ego—working alone or in tandem with paid professionals to keep the brother or sister out of harm's way. The choices they face are agonizing. For Rachel Simon it means authorizing sterilization for a sexually active retarded sister who—despite a love for babies—is deemed unable to care for a child. Jay Neugeboren, as many others whose siblings are mentally ill, must select from an array of insufficient options in housing arrangements, medications, and caretakers. Geographical separation and the vacillating moods of siblings make the decisions all the more difficult.[2]

It never gets easier. In fact, repetition of similar issues over time solidifies the authors' initial feelings of survivor's guilt and conflict over their role. Neugeboren writes: "I find myself wondering again . . ." (*Imagining Robert*, 44). Simon writes: "I will always wrestle with the notion of . . . " (*Riding the Bus with My Sister*, 284). Again and always, they are their siblings' keepers.

The situation is quite different for authors who grew apart from siblings once both were grown, and before the sibling encountered difficulty. They started out in life on an even playing field. There was no history of disparate abilities in their childhood homes, no reason for concern if weeks, even months passed without getting in touch. They were busy—living in different worlds. And they were all healthy young adults. There was plenty of time.

Now the brother or sister is in a serious medical crisis that is destined to end in premature death: cancer, HIV/AIDS, a critical accident. Authors search their memories and come up with memories of childhood closeness. Older siblings remember their brothers and sisters as new babies they treated as dolls. Younger siblings recall looking up to their brothers and sisters—wanting to be like them in every way. When and why did everything change?

Often it is a matter of social class. J. D. Dolan wrote: "In my brother's world, people bought new engines. In my world, people bought new cars" (*Phoenix*, 151). The author who had been close to a sibling in childhood went on to higher education, to higher income, to interests that the brother or sister did not share. After a few failed efforts to bridge the gap, it seemed easier to let the separation stand.

Linked to social class but distinct from it is a difference in worldview. Jamaica Kincaid and Barbara Lazear Ascher were not only geographically separated from their younger brothers but worlds apart in their ideas of what constitutes a good life. They were not judgmental of the sexual practices that resulted in their brothers contracting HIV/AIDS; rather it was the context in which these practices take place—a casual, hedonistic approach to life, so at odds with their own more traditional choices—that was difficult for them to accept.

Yet even when siblings grow up to share the same values, interests, and a continuing affection, jobs in distant locales or idiosyncratic situations are responsible for an emotional separation. Alan Shapiro's father cast his daughter Beth out of the family after she married a black man. Devotion to his sister and outrage over this treatment notwithstanding, Shapiro continued a relationship with their parents—conflicting allegiances that reverberated in the sibling relationship.

Filled with regret over lost opportunities for closeness, they gather at the bedside, doing what they can, trying to make up for lost time. They are often able to offer concrete resources and emotional support. However, the emotional breach between siblings is rarely bridged before death. Later, at gravesites and in the privacy of their own worlds once again, they think back on the relationship and mourn what never was.

It is at this point that the path of the authors who first begin to consider the sibling relationship at the point of a medical crisis joins that of the authors who have had a lifetime to reflect upon it.

For many authors the memoir reflects internal conflicts. Clifford Chase wrote: "Even now, five years later, I want to stop and turn to the jury and say, 'See: See what I was up against?' And still I want to be the hero of the story—of a simple story, in which I offer the right answer and it's rejected" (*A Hurry Up Song*, 100).

It is never a simple story and there are no heroes. Whether the memoir ends with impaired siblings still alive or ill siblings now dead, the past cannot be redone. Internal debates and unresolved feelings are a part of the authors' lives from now on. Like Barbara Lazear Ascher, they may lament, "If only I had been an extraordinary rather than an ordinary sister" (*Landscape Without Gravity*, 116). Yet simply classifying one's past actions as "ordinary" rather than loathsome is a step in the direction of self-forgiveness.

In tales of sibling care, self-justification and keening regret reflect the guilt of living on, unimpaired, more sharply than in any other family relationships. As J. D. Dolan wrote, "And while my brother lay dying in a burn unit, I felt terribly, guiltily, hungrily alive" (*Phoenix*, 80).

Peer support groups, the passing of time, and the writing of the memoir itself—all are accredited by the authors with helping them separate themselves from their siblings and accept the right to the life that awaits them.

# chapter 9

## Couple Care

### "This Terrible Traffic Regulation"

[A husband writes:] "This cold truth, this terrible traffic regulation ('You, Madam, to the right—you, Sir, to the left') is just the beginning of the separation which is death itself."
—C. S. Lewis, *A Grief Observed*, 30

Out of all the people they might have chosen to spend their lives with, they picked each other. They forged an intimate partnership—of which sexual intimacy was both expression and symbol. Then one of them became seriously ill, and now the other is telling their story.

Little things matter in shared lives: daily routines, small pleasures, idiosyncratic preferences and irritations known only to each other. Anticipated loss of a cherished way of life and efforts to preserve as much of it as possible for as long as possible infuse the memoirs of couple care. Told in parallel narratives of "we" and "I," the story reflects the split identity of the authors—now as part of a team facing adversity together, now as individuals up against the "traffic regulation" that dictates a parting of their ways.

The path is long and torturous, a cumulative progression of losses and the portent of final loss. Against a backdrop of how the pair met, their decision to cast their lot together, and their lives before the health crisis, the authors tell of multiple challenges: disclosing the situation and handling the reactions of others, the continuous process of adaptation to a relationship where everything from the tasks of daily living and leisure-time activities through sexuality, child care, and financial management has to be periodically reconfigured. In each of these activities, the authors share a common concern: that, no matter how diminished their capacities may be, their partners be accorded all the respect due fully functioning human beings. An emphasis on upholding the dignity and personhood of the partner against the endemic and gratuitous assaults of illness and approaching death is, indeed, the hallmark of couple care. For in honoring their partners' integrity, the authors preserve their own.

Maggie Strong expresses an ambivalence that is shared by many authors: "If you tell, folks gather round with love and cookies, and you'll need all of that you can get. But once the word is out, people will look at you differently and you'll feel different too" (*Mainstay*, 52). When it comes to the illness of a partner, disclosure is a problem not only in the case of stigmatized illnesses: no condition is exempt from the fear of telling. Going public with a private matter marks a point of no return.

Unless the health situation is self-evident, deciding what others have to know and when they have to know it is a major concern for young and middle-aged couples. Broadsided by an unexpected catastrophe while in the midst of active work, family, and social lives, they can hardly take in the implications themselves. What of their parents, who will be devastated? How will they reassure their frightened children? When must employers be informed? Which friends can they rely on and which friends will turn away?

Older couples, who may be retired and at a time of life when illness or disability is more expected, are less guarded. Still, they remain protective of grown children, aged siblings, and friends. Most important, they are fearful of losing autonomy by letting others in.

No matter what the age or situation of the couple, they are treated by the world as a unit. Attitudes toward one invariably affect the other. Breaking the news, being and feeling "different" is the first step in a process of dealing with the outside world that will last for the length of the illness. With every instance where a partner is not visited by family and friends because "it's too painful to see him like this" or "I want to remember her as she was" (common responses in cases of cancer or advanced dementia), the author becomes more isolated. Persistent phone inquiries to inquire about the partner, pat cautions to the author to take care of herself, and people who glibly ask to be notified "if there's anything I can do" come in for particularly scathing commentary. (Alternatives—such as seeing a need and filling it without asking, and visiting in pairs so one can stay with the ill partner while the other takes the well partner out for a few hours—are suggested.)

Yet even as they bemoan the sense of isolation, most authors—whether they are young, middle-aged, or old, gay or straight, facing cancer, Alzheimer's HIV/AIDS, dementia, or a progressive paralyzing illness—express a comfortable sense of being alone together. Closer now than ever before. Two against the world.

These two contradictory impulses—cherishing a deepening bond with the partner while chafing against a steady erosion of previous forms of socialization—are typical of couple care. Martha Weinman Lear writes: "There were many things we could no longer do, none crucial to our well-being, but we did miss them: no theater, no museums, no large parties, no explorations about town; everything planned by the pills, the clock and the availability of emergency help. Now the most modest outings seemed festive" (*Heartsounds*, 250).

Feelings of deprivation echo through the memoirs. When the illness is fatal, these feelings are shuffled aside. Aware that their days together are numbered, authors concentrate their efforts on celebrating what remains. But when the illness is chronic, authors experience an uncomfortable emotional mix: anger at one's own isolation mingled with guilt, and compassion for the worse condition of the partner.

Authors detail the household responsibilities newly assumed and former pleasures no longer possible. Anticipating an indefinite future promising more of the same, they stop short of self-pity. Resignation and a desire to turn the experience into some good for others usually result—of which the memoir is one manifestation.

Social activism is another. Maggie Strong, a young woman whose husband had multiple sclerosis, was the first to identify herself as a "well spouse," and in so doing started a powerful self-help movement by recognizing that caregiving husbands and wives may have different needs than their ill partners. Beverly Bigtree Murphy, an older woman whose spouse had Alzheimer's Disease, became a public speaker on the topic. Morton Kondrake, whose wife had Parkinson's Disease, became a lobbyist and advocate for increased funding and research.

All of the authors were able to put other responsibilities on hold for the duration of a health-care crisis—such as emergency hospitalization or surgery. Few (the retired or self-employed) tell of being together round-the-clock for an open-ended period of time. Putting individual interests on hold for the duration, they subsume themselves in the care of their partners. Such private time as they manage is in some way related to this care—such as attending support groups or writing in the journals that are forerunners of the memoir before us.

Gender—as well as the financial necessity for gainful employment—plays an important role in determining who will spend time apart from an ailing partner, for how long, and for what purpose. There is no question that Milton Kondrake, a political commentator, and Stanley Winawer, a physician, will spend the daytime hours away from home, continuing to work in their professions, while others care for their ill wives. However, Gerda Lerner is advised by her husband's physician that she should leave her academic work to care for him in the final stages of cancer—and it is with a great effort of will that she contradicts this expectation.

Working partners do not shun responsibilities at home. What with coordinating the home health aides and covering for the inevitable gaps and lapses in care, they are often more stressed than those spouses who devote full time to the effort. However, time apart is a source of comfort, reminding them of the strengths and pleasures they can still enjoy as individuals.

Still, it is the life together that has changed and is mourned. Preserving what was, through a fierce clinging to the "normal" and maintaining past habits and rituals, becomes the goal. As Jean Craig wrote: "Our salvation was not going to be found in the noble virtue of courage, but in the everyday succor of normalcy" (*Between Hello and Goodbye*, 23). Although authors watch their partners closely for an increase of symptoms, they resist the urge to treat them as patients. They take pride in treating them as they always have.

Appetites may flag and—short of offering foods that tempt the palate—they decide, like Nancy Rossi, whose husband is in a terminal stage of cancer, not to check up on how much of the meal served was actually consumed. Limited diets may be called for, and authors like Janice Burns, whose husband has HIV/AIDS, choose to eat theirs in another room so their partners will not have to see the widening gulf between them. Consciously eschewing the infantilization that often overcomes professional caregivers when dealing with intimate body functions of dependent patients, they demonstrate mutuality in the smallest of actions.

Clothes and shoes, hair and makeup—subjects hardly mentioned in other relationships—assume importance in memoirs of couple care. Husbands and wives of Alzheimer's patients (with the exception of John Bayley, who candidly admits an obliviousness to such matters) work hard to keep up the physical appearances of their partners—even when bathing, dressing, and grooming consume an inordinate amount of time and effort. Observing that the body of her husband has shrunk inside his once-fitting clothes is a source of pain to Martha Weinman Lear, whose husband suffers from advanced heart disease. Nancy Rossi sees to her husband's comfort by providing a jogging suit while Janice Burns, whose husband has HIV/AIDS, takes care that his work clothes are up to par. Morton Kondrake delights in the care his wheelchair-bound wife still maintains in her appearance.

All find some way to connect a diminished present with memories of their shared past. As Bayley writes, "One needs very much to feel that the unique individuality of one's spouse has not been lost in the common symptoms of a clinical condition" (*Elegy for Iris*, 49). Rituals may be altered or new rituals may be substituted for old. Burton Wheeler and his wife, who suffers from Alzheimer's Disease, still enjoy a "cocktail" before dinner although hers is no longer alcoholic and the lively conversation that accompanied it is no longer possible. John Bayley and his wife, Iris, can't swim together anymore, but they can watch the Teletubbies on television. Sidney Winawer and his wife, who has cancer, spend less time discussing the trivialities of life, more time appreciating the moment and studying the Bible.

Above all, authors strive to maintain an equality in their relationship. Gerda Lerner writes of her husband's last days: "I would not cripple him any more than he was already crippled. As long as he, of his own free will, could do something for me, even just by giving me some time for myself, he was still himself, the man he had always been" (*A Death of One's Own*, 64).

A history of reciprocity, along with a sexual history, separates the situation of partners from other family care relationships. And although most authors draw the curtain when it comes to sharing details of their intimate life, they devote considerable space to chronicling the earlier give-and-take that cemented their bond. It may have been dramatic—Kondrake was on the road to becoming an alcoholic before his wife's intervention. But more often it is the interest in the other's career, the support at hard moments, the sage advice, the sharing of care for aged parents and dependent children. Finding new ways for the partner to reciprocate—like altering or substituting rituals—is another way that normality is preserved. It may mean redefining "doing something for me," as Lerner notes. Or it may mean collaborating on a new project in which they can share equal status: Edmund White and his partner, who is ill with HIV/AIDS, decide to publish a book about the Paris that they love, with White doing the text and Sorin doing the illustrations. Openly gay, they celebrate the same-sex attraction that brought them together without going into specifics of their private lives.

The few authors who write of sexual intimacy display a range of circumstances and emotions. Reflecting upon how his sex life has changed since the advent of his wife's illness, Wheeler writes: "One doesn't make love. One discovers and shares it" (*Close to Me But Far Away*, 150). Although he still feels desire and she passively accepts his advances, he cannot bear the thought that he is forcing himself upon her, ceasing sexual intercourse when she is past the stage of discovery and sharing. Pats, hugs, and terms of endearment will have to suffice. On the other hand, Beverly Murphy's husband—also afflicted with Alzheimer's Disease—retains his sexual zeal well into the course of the illness and the bond is a source of comfort to both of them. Janice Burns, who contracted HIV/AIDS from her husband before either of them knew his status, does not hold him responsible for the illness they share; nevertheless, their sexual relationship is tainted by the knowledge of how their fate was transmitted. Then there is Gerda Lerner, who cherishes the memory of the last time she and her husband made love, thirty days before his death: "Amazingly, he spoke to me with his body the way he had always spoken" (257).

The reticence about discussing sexual consequences of a partner's illness—and the variety of responses when it is discussed—is matched by the way relationships with children are portrayed. Maggie Strong wrote: "Were the kids spending the day away from home or alone in their rooms because they were teenagers? Or were they escaping the gloom of the house? There wasn't time to figure it out. Where does it hurt? The whole house hurts, the couch curtains are swollen with pain, the rugs flat with despair" (149).

Authors who have children rarely speak for or about them. A wish to protect their privacy, a fear of appropriating their story is palpable though not explicitly stated. When children are mentioned, this is usually limited to cameo appearances. Small children are said to be in the care of neighbors or relatives. Teenage children are described as off with friends. Grown children are usually portrayed as occupied with work and their own families.

Bucking the general trend of glossing over difficulties are a few authors who explicitly present what others only infer—that the serious illness and anticipated or actual death of a parent is a critical event in the life of children whatever their age. In an effort to help her children express the feelings they seem to be running from, Maggie Strong seeks family therapy. Nancy Rossi prepares a scrapbook of memories for the infant son who will never know his father. One of Jean Craig's children from a first marriage moves in to help with the terminal care of her stepfather. As for the rest, they are seen but not heard, caring but distant figures in the ongoing dramas between their parents. Dramas that wend their way to memoir's end.

Recalling the lengthy hospitalization of her husband, Molly Haskell wrote, "More and more I felt a sense of amputation" (*Love and Other Infectious Diseases*, 155). Ironically, she is the only author of a couple-care memoir whose partner fully recovered. Yet she expresses the sense of all the authors: those who are still in the midst of caring and those who are mourning the death of a partner at memoir's end. A piece of them is missing. Nevertheless, their lives go on.

In memoirs of chronic illnesses, the authors speak of slowly coming to terms with the "traffic regulation," finding an equilibrium between their needs and those of the partner—a life apart, a life together. They discover and cultivate sources of individual solace and find a way to balance it with their commitment to a partner. Some insert stories of other partners they have known or heard of who could not stay the course: trumped up a nonillness related reason for a separation or placed their partners in a nursing home when home care was still possible. Quick to say that they are not judging, recognizing that each situation is different—and that they may one day be driven to just such a move—it is nonetheless clear that they take pride in their efforts to do all they can, that the sacrifice of their energies (especially in the case of elderly spouses) is more than matched by the reward of knowing they have done the best that they could.

Several memoirs of couple care focus primarily on survival after the death of the partner. Written several years after the loss—and generally reconstructed from journals or notes written at the time—they speak eloquently of death and healing, often in the present tense. They write of the beginning stages. Sandy Broyard, whose husband died of cancer, writes, "Losing my husband is like losing who I am. It is losing the texture, the denseness, the three-dimensional quality of my life. Now I am only flat. I am no longer me" (*Standby*, 17). They write of the difficulty of getting through the days, of the slow, painful dismantling of closets, of houses, of friendships—and the equally slow process of building new lives and new relationships.

Stories about life after a partner has died depend to a large degree on the life stage of the author and on the time between the loss and the writing of the memoir. Although the mourning of young and mid-life authors is deep and long-lasting, they express an openness to the possibility of new relationships that is not present in memoirs of older spouses. Yet in describing death's aftermath all would concur with Fenton Johnson, writing years after his partner's death from AIDS: "It is years later, I am here and he is not but love goes on, this is the lesson that I have taken, for a comfort that must and will suffice. In grief there is renewal, of love and so of life" (*Geography of the Heart*, 237).

# chapter 10
## Parent Care

### "The Consummate Act"

If she died while I was unable to mourn for her, I felt that I would
wipe out her existence as a mother . . . while at the same time I would
diminish my own life in a way I couldn't yet understand. . . . A child
needs parents to give him life and nurture him—but a father or mother has an equally urgent need for a child to complete the parent's life
and give him a proper death through the consummate act of seeing
him whole.
—Joan Gould, *Spirals*, 5

Leaving home is the classic coming-of-age plot. It happens after all
kinds of childhoods, in all kinds of families. College and jobs, new
intimacies and interests, moves across town, country, the world—all
are tickets out. Whether the distance is geographic or emotional, a
brief adolescent rebellion or a years-long estrangement, adult children maintain a delicate balance between their new worlds and the
ones they left behind. Until once-independent mothers and fathers
begin to fail—or ever-vulnerable parents worsen. The equilibrium is
shattered. And they return to pick up where they left off.[1]

Years, usually decades, have passed since the authors spent so
much time in their parents' company—or so much time thinking
about them when they are apart. The authors are no longer the children they were; they have spent some time out in the world, learning

about others and about themselves. Their parents too have changed. However strong their personalities remain, the ravages of aging and illness have reduced their power.

Most important, the relationship itself has changed. It is not—as some suggest—a "role reversal" (although the adult child might perform tasks for the parent that the parent once performed for her, their shared past can never be erased). Rather it is a new kind of intimacy, one infused with a need to know their parents as individuals in their own right, to see them "whole."

The leitmotif of parent-care memoirs is separation and return—weaving over, under, and through widely disparate family constellations and situations to construct a universal tale. Although sibling relationships, the impact of the adult child's age, and a confrontation with family secrets are commonly shared themes, it is the road home that sets parent-care memoirs apart from those of other family relationships. Whether the road is short or long, what begins as a return to care ends with the claiming of the author's genetic and psychic legacy. Seeing the parent "whole" is seen as finding a missing piece of oneself. As the parents of a newborn try to discern which of the baby's features are "from" the mother and which "from" the father, authors create meaning by finding themselves in their parents and their parents in themselves.

Many authors are only children, yet no generalization about the meaning of this status can be made from the memoirs. Their adult relationships with parents run the gamut from adoring to estranged, with every permutation in between. Indeed the variety to be found in their memoirs gives the lie to any theory that theirs is inherently an easier or more difficult situation.

Linda Grant, whose memoir was of caring for a mother with multi-infarct dementia, invited her sister to write a chapter and recognized: "My greatest debt is to my sister, Michele Grant, without whose permission there would have been no book. Who went through exactly what I did and whose story this is as well as mine, though each of us would tell it differently according to our own point of view" (*Remind Me Who I Am, Again*, 300). Among the authors who have siblings are several who mention them only when it advances or explains the story line. Philip Roth—whose brother's inability to get to the hospital in time enabled him to be alone at his father's deathbed—is a prime example. Whether authors do this to protect the privacy of the relationship or to maintain the focus of the narrative is unclear. Of the sibling relationships that are depicted in detail, only one is openly hostile—that of Brenda Avadian, whose disagreement with her brothers over how best to care for their father escalates into a complete breakdown of communication among them. Most authors describe the period of parent care as a renewal or deepening of a childhood bond with brothers and sisters.

Leaving home may mean a separation from siblings as well as from parents. The title of T. M. Shine's memoir—*Fathers Aren't Supposed to Die: Five Brothers Reunite to Say Goodbye*—speaks to a commonly expressed experience. Regret at the years when they could have been closer mingles with appreciation of rediscovering one another as adults.

Cooperation—often involving a synchronized division of labor—is the rule. Male siblings, like Christopher Dickey and his brother, were more likely to handle instrumental tasks, like finances and decision making. Sisters found a way to share hands-on, daily tasks. The memoirs of Simone de Beauvoir and Marion Roach, as well as that of Linda Grant, attest to the power of such partnerships. The male-female differentiation of tasks also holds true when there are siblings of two genders—such as Martin Amis, whose sister and mother provide hands-on care, and Eleanor Cooley, whose brother manages finances.

The opportunity to share early memories with siblings is cited as a positive aspect of the parent-care experience. A generosity of spirit infuses the belated recognition that one's siblings had a different experience with the parent growing up and in adulthood now has (as Linda Grant put it) her own "point of view."

Conventional wisdom has it that parent care is a task of the middle years—of an inelegantly dubbed "sandwich generation" who find themselves squeezed between the demands of growing children and ailing elders. Memoirs are a reminder that the call may well come to those who are under the age of thirty or over the age of seventy. Authors at these stages of life are facing developmental issues that influence the care they can offer their parents and the meanings they create out of the experience. Marion Roach, who was in her early twenties when her mother was diagnosed with Alzheimer's Disease, wrote: "I had always imagined that on the day, whenever it was—that I had my first success, however, I judged it, I would have someone, a parent most specifically, there to coo. . . . My mother didn't know anything about it, my father was dead" (*Another Name for Madness*, 161).

The young are still trying to separate from their parents. Bound up in their own struggle for independence, they are not yet able to recognize their mothers and fathers as individuals apart from their parental role. In time, these authors might have matured into to an adult-to-adult relationship with their parents, accepting of their differences, perhaps even admiring their unique qualities. The unanticipated illness or accident denied them of that opportunity. Like Rodger Kamenetz and Dani Shapiro, they may belatedly return. Like Nathaniel Lachenmeyer or Julie Hilden, they might not make it back in time. Whatever their degree of involvement at the time of their parent's last illness, these authors share a lifelong sorrow. Each professional and personal success reawakens the sense of loss—their parents are not there to share it; they never had the opportunity to make their parents proud.

In contrast to the many young memoir authors, there are only two who are old. And they bear an amazing similarity. Lillian Rubin and Allan Wheelis are both over seventy, both psychoanalysts who have spent professional lifetimes exploring the mother-child relationship; yet personal resolution eludes them. Although they continue to feel resentment over their early lives and have their own health problems, they do what they can to ease the lives of their centenarian mothers. Unlike young and mid-life authors, for them the parent-care experience inevitably resonates with intimations of their own deterioration and death.

Parent care often awakens curiosity in children about parts of their parents' lives unknown to them. Charles Pierce, whose father had Alzheimer's Disease, wrote: "In many ways, I grew up knowing more about the marriage of Abraham and Mary Todd Lincoln than I did about the marriage of John and Patricia Pierce, who, as far as I knew, had appeared on this earth, fully grown, shortly before my birth" (*Hard to Forget*, xx). Who *were* one's parents? What were their lives before one was born? Did they love each other? Recognizing one's mother or father as an individual—with abilities, motivations, and conflicts that had nothing to do with oneself—is for many authors an unanticipated by-product of the parent-care experience.

With parent care come more occasions for observation, more opportunities for reminiscence. Looking through photograph albums, hearing new stories, and rehearing old ones forces a new perspective on a parents identity and one's own. It is a bittersweet time—gratitude at finally knowing, regret at not knowing sooner. Hillary Johnson and Alex Kates Shulman learn that their mothers had greater depths, more talents than they had ever appreciated. Ted Solotaroff learns that his father's brutal behavior toward him was the product of his own deprived upbringing.

The memoirs describe many instances of serial care (one parent falling ill soon after the other died) and simultaneous care (of mother and father). Several help one parent in the care of the other. As did Alex Shulman, C. K. Williams, and LeAnne Schreiber, they observed an interaction between their now-aged parents that sometimes echoed, sometimes contradicted, what they previously believed. A father who disappeared from the scene (through divorce, desertion, or death) many years before casts a long shadow. Already idealized, the occasions of a mother's illness are reason for the fathers to be mourned anew by the daughters—like Jackie Lyden and Mary Gordon—they left behind.

There is much to assimilate. Old stories resonate with new meanings. Vague surmisings are filled out with facts. Parents who were married to other people before the union that produced the author and extramarital affairs (a few resulting in other children) are emotionally charged concerns shared by several authors. Then there are the mental health or criminal histories of more distant relatives whose existence had always been recognized though their names were rarely spoken. All are not new revelations—but for the first time the authors have the time and space to ponder their meanings.

Each new bit of information whets the appetite for more. Most intriguing is family history. Reaching as far into the past as they can—memories and stories of great-grandparents and grandparents—authors recount what they now know about both sides of the family from whence they came. Tracing those histories—the meeting that introduced their parents to one another, and all the years that came after when their love waxed and waned—is a goal sought but rarely achieved. On the outside, looking in, they can only surmise.

Alex Kates Shulman, who once believed that having an independent life meant severing close bonds with her mother and father, wrote: "Not till my parents were dead did I recognize escape as a leap on the long road home" (*The Good Enough Daughter*, xiii–xiv). The memoirs suggest that "the long road home" is actually four separate roads—ranging from the shortest (adult children who were born to a mentally or physically impaired parents and cannot remember a time when they were *not* involved in care) to the longest (adult children who had out of contact with parents for years before their final illness).

The first group of authors could be called "born to care." Growing up in a home where those who are supposed to look after you need help themselves leaves a lifelong mark. In many ways, the early lives of these authors resemble those who grew up with impaired siblings. Embarrassed over having a mother or father who is visibly different from the parents of their peers, needing to act as adults when they want to act like children, protecting the inside life of the family from the curious gaze of the outside world. Lou Ann Walker wrote, "I was an adult before I was a child. . . . Outside our house speaking and hearing seemed to be valued more than anything. And that is what we had nothing of at home. I was the child who did all my parents' business transactions, nearly from the time I was a toddler. I spoke for my parents; I heard for my parents" (*A Loss for Words*, 2).

Parents who were deaf, physically crippled, or mentally ill arouse a host of warring emotions. Anger at being cheated of "normal" parents jostles with the knowledge that their parents suffered still more. Pride at one's own accomplishments can never be felt without that stab of recognition that one's parents lacked the capacity for such achievement. Living one's own life was not easy for those who left dependent parents behind. Some stayed closely involved. Some tried to keep a distance. Most wove back and forth: duty and compassion at odds with the need to break free.

Some tried to complete in their own lives the paths that their parents could not. Jackie Lyden's life was a study in motion and risk: she performed in a rodeo, then appeared on public radio, reporting on trouble spots around the world—acting out the adventurous life that was the stuff of her mother's delusions. Sherwin B. Nuland could not cure his father or make up for the losses of his life, but became a physician who could heal others. Many authors with dependent parents maintained a connection to the past even as they moved out of its orbit. Years after Lou Ann Walker graduated from Harvard and established a literary career, she continued to do volunteer work with the deaf.

For these authors, parent care at the end of life is a continuation of all that had gone before—with a difference. Now working and raising families of their own, they realize—in a way they never have before—how hard life was for their parents. Imbued with a new appreciation of all that their parents achieved in spite of the limitations on their lives, they find that their anger is tempered. After years of struggle—often abetted by psychotherapy—they are able to take pride in their own achievements without guilt. Through their choice of helping professions, through the writing of the memoir itself, they pay homage.

A second group of authors could be called "the adoring." When her mother was dying of cancer, LeAnne Schreiber wanted to communicate her feelings to the nursing aides: "I took a picture out of my purse, a picture of Mom and me looking eternally young in Rome last summer, and placed it on her bedside table. . . I wanted them to see that she had been them, is still one of them, even now, when she is so nearly invisible. I hoped to seduce them into kindness, with her beauty and her life" (*Midstream*, 266). Adoring children saw their mothers and fathers as friends. It was not that they were emotionally arrested in childhood and unable to move on. Or that they felt compelled to share everything about their private lives. Just that they cherished every memory, every day that they spent with their parents and found it hard to envision a world without them.

These authors often recall a brief passing phase of adolescent separation, followed by decades of emotional closeness and mutual admiration. From an early age, they showed an interest in family history and memorabilia. They cherished old stories. Philip Roth and Calvin Trillin tried to transfer all of their fathers' early experiences to their own memory banks. While adoring children have usually exceeded their parents in education and worldly success, they feel that their mothers and fathers embodied qualities that matter more: devotion to family, hard work, courage.

What unites the authors who sustained an adoring attitude toward their parents throughout their adult lives is not a matter of gender— they are evenly divided. Nor is it an idyllic childhood (though most seem to see the past through rose-colored glasses). One theme virtually leaps from every page: these adult children have always felt *themselves* to be adored. Added to this are continuously reinforcing experiences—concrete and emotional support that continues long after their adult children leave home. Betty Rollin recalls awakening after her own cancer surgery to see her mother arranging the flowers in her room and being flooded with a sense of comfort and well-being.

When their parents need care in late life, these adult children do not have far to travel. However great the geographic distance, they are already emotionally close to home. Watching a beloved parent deteriorate and die causes a wound that is deep but clean. Memories of the past bring comfort—as do the physical objects (photographs, personal effects, furnishings) that embody them.

A third group of authors could be called "the estranged." Christopher Dickey writes of his father, the author James Dickey: "For most of twenty years I did not see him, couldn't talk to him, could not bear to be around him. . . . It was a cold knot of anger that . . . helped drive me to do the things I wanted and needed to do in my own life. . . . Anger was so much easier to deal with than love" (*Summer of Deliverance*, 13). They had their reasons. Parents who were alcoholic, competitive, rejecting. Parents who they felt would smother their attempts at independence. Parents they could never please. Overwhelmed, angry, or simply avoiding a repeat of unpleasant situations, these adult children made the break as soon as they were able and stayed away as long as they could.

Sometimes they returned in the nick of time. Christopher Dickey blamed his alcoholic and philandering father for the alcohol-related death of his mother. He married while still in his teens and got a job as a foreign correspondent on the other side of the world. By the time he returned, his father was in desperate shape—the family home a shambles, his second marriage a disaster, alcoholic hepatitis bringing his health to the edge of no return. In the few months before his father's death, father and son are able to reclaim relics of their family life and revive memories of the days before the horrors began.

Some authors returned too late. It was only after his father's death that Nathaniel Lachenmeyer felt a curiosity to find out about his life. It was only after her mother's death that Julie Hilden felt the weight of her neglect. However damaged the parents' life, authors searched among the ruins for bits that they could claim. Dickey's memoir includes a bibliography of his father's works and a transcript of his last lecture. Lachenmeyer interviewed everyone who knew his father during his final years and discovered him as a person who maintained hope and faith in life against all odds.

In their books, the authors redeem their father's reputations; and in so doing, learn to forgive themselves for the time apart. This is not the case for Julie Hilden, however, whose book title—*The Bad Daughter*—reflects the legacy of her inaction.

Larger than all the other groups combined is that containing the authors who could be called "home for the holidays" adult children. They kept in touch and were everywhere they were expected to be, but they did not tarry. Their lives were otherwise engaged—often in defining themselves as different from the parents who had raised them. It was a choice they lived to regret. And in their memoirs they tell us of that regret and how they sought to reverse it. Simone de Beauvoir wrote: "When someone you love dies you pay for the sin of outliving her with a thousand piercing regrets. . . . With regard to Maman we were above all guilty, these last years, of carelessness, omission, abstention. We felt that we atoned for this by the days we gave up to her, by the peace our victories gained over fear and pain. Without our obstinate watchfulness, she would have suffered far more" (*A Very Easy Death*, 108).

Women authors who came of age in the 1960s (and de Beauvoir, who blazed the trail two decades before) defined themselves by the distance they had come from the traditional world of their mothers. If they decided to marry, it was not for financial security or social acceptance. If they stayed married or had children it was not for want of other options. They worked outside the home as a matter of course and took it as a given that the only limits on their professional advancement came from within themselves. They did not stifle their own opinions in order to be agreeable; they did not amuse themselves with arts projects, gossip, and card games. Some of these daughters recall idolizing their mothers when they were young. They date the rift to adolescence, when they discovered new ways of thinking and acting, intellectual and sexual freedoms that forged a wall between them. Some daughters were still in thrall to childhood hurts and rejections. They all maintained contact—although frequency did not necessarily reflect a warmth of feeling.

The generational divide is different for most of the male authors. When they had sisters and wives to keep family ties alive, little was expected of them beyond making an appearance at family occasions and helping out in family emergencies—which they did willingly. Sometimes they were flooded with warm feelings for their parents, but it was nothing to dwell upon. They were not haunted by miserable childhoods or nostalgic for idyllic ones. After all, they had jobs and families of their own.

For men and women who had given cursory attention to their parents through most of their adulthood, care during the last years of their lives is seen as an atonement for years in which they could and should have paid more attention. They find meaning in the acknowledgment of what was lost and the salvaging of what remained.

In the memoirs, all roads home ended in one place: the death of the parent or parents and its aftermath for the author. Funeral scenes and eulogies abound in memoirs of parent care—as does the disbursement of a mother or father's personal belongings. Authors are often taken by surprise at how attached they are to these objects. Ted Solotaroff wrote: "Most of all, given my bitter memories of his business, which had cost me part of my youth, why had I taken away an old glass cutter I'd found in the basement of his house, and put it in the jar on my desk that holds pens, pencils, and felt markers, the tools of my trade?" (*Truth Comes in Blows*, 48). Artifacts of lost parents become totems—carried back from the parent-care experience to enrich the authors' ongoing lives. Household furnishings, personal effects of a mother or father—now mingling with one's own—are emblematic of the claimed legacy.

One author after another traces the lineage of personality traits. Janet Farrington Graham writes: "I recognize her fear in my quickness to ride a wave of impatience or build a wall of anger. I recognize her love in my eagerness to forgive the occasional pain caused by family and friends. . . . They have been tempered by an endowment of common sense from my father" (*Letters to Harry*, 200). Alex Kates Shulman writes: "Mom's sensuality and will, Dad's rationality and focus—are, like my parents themselves, the source of what I am" (253). In their words, in their gestures, in the resemblance to a parent they glimpse through their own images in the mirror, the authors find comfort in similarities that might once have been jarring.

At the death of her mother Madeleine L'Engle wrote, "The pattern has shifted; we have changed places in the dance. I am no longer anybody's child. I have become the Grandmother. . . . The rhythm of the fugue alters: the themes cross and recross. The melody seems unfamiliar to me, but I will learn it" (*The Summer of the Great-Grandmother*, 243). Few transitions are as seamless as that of L'Engle, who can trace her matriarchal line back for seven generations. Yet most authors with children (especially those with grandchildren) feel that they have, indeed, changed places in the "dance."

And many authors do not have children. But completing the trajectory—not only from the past to the present but from the present to the future—is a coda to most of the memoirs of the parent-care relationship. Through their relationships with others, through their work itself—of which the book before us is a prime example—the legacy lives on.

# part 3

## The Memoirs

It is our inward journey that leads us through time—forward or back, seldom in a straight line, most often spiraling. Each of us is moving, changing, with respect to others. As we discover, we remember; remembering, we discover.
—Eudora Welty

# chapter 11
## Introduction
### "Jointly Human"

> Reading, haven't we often encountered a passage that captured per-
> fectly a moment in our own lives? Mightn't we collect these and thus
> demonstrate the sameness of our lives? . . .We could demonstrate in
> this way not the differences between lives but their sameness, their
> commonness, their comforting banality. . . . Might not it be the case
> that we are jointly human instead of merely animals of the same spe-
> cies?
> —William Gass (1994, 51)

Maybe you can't tell a book by its cover. But if you put the cover together with drawings and photographs, typesets and fonts, quotes
and guest chapters, epilogues and appendixes, you can tell quite a
lot. The book as object—title, jacket, and promotional endorsements
included—tells a story all its own. Memoir titles are often lengthy,
double-barreled affairs, reflecting the publisher's effort to show that
although the author's story is sad, reading it need not be depressing.

Although many memoirs are based upon journal entries, there is
great variety in how these entries are used. A few authors trumpet
the fact that they are presenting unedited, unamplified notes written
while they were in the midst of the situation. Some authors juxtapose
these entries with retrospective views on the event (typically using
italics to differentiate between the two) while others acknowledge

that their journals are mere jogs to the memory. The majority of authors simply write the story as they choose to recall it—with what Mishler (1995, 90) terms "the telling and the told" intertwined in a way that makes sense to them now.[1]

A memoir can be the finely crafted composition of a literary master, who may in fact have treated the same themes in fiction. Writing about the care of a brain-damaged son is a Nobel Laureate in literature, Kenzaburo Oë. Writing about the care of a mother with cancer is a renowned cultural figure of the twentieth century, Simone de Beauvoir. A memoir may read like a journalistic exposé, an advocacy manifesto, or a scenario for a "disease of the week" television special. There are memoirs as relentlessly chronological as week-at-a-glance diaries, and memoirs that draw graceful figure eights through space and time. Then there are the hybrids—the author's personal story intertwined with "how to" tips and resource guides. Memoirs resist a simple definition.

Sometimes the memoir author invites a care partner to contribute to the book. John Gunther's memoir includes a chapter by his ex-wife, who shared the care of their teenage son as he died of cancer. Linda Grant's sister has the last word in the story of their mother, who suffered from multi-infarct dementia.

Sometimes the ill or disabled family member shares in authorship. Brooke and Jean Ellison are a mother and daughter who write alternate sections of a memoir about life after the automobile accident that left the daughter paraplegic. Hydeia and Patricia Broadbent, another mother and the daughter she adopted in infancy, take turns telling the story of a child born with AIDS as she grows into adolescence.

Even when ill or disabled family members are unable to write a substantial portion of the memoir, some authors try to give them a voice. Paul McDonnell, who is autistic, and Seth Kramer, who has cerebral palsy, each contribute an "afterword" to his mother's book about caring for him. Lauren Manning, a burn victim of September 11, writes a postscript to her husband's story of her recovery. Hubert Sorin, who died of HIV/AIDS, participates in his lover's memoir through his drawings, which punctuate the text.

Several memoirs are printed on glossy paper—the better to show-case family artwork. Clara Claiborne Park reproduces paintings by her autistic daughter. Kenzaburo Oë features drawings that his wife made of their family as they cared for their brain-damaged son. The contribution of Hillary Johnson's mother, Ruth, is acknowledged on the memoir's cover and her artwork fills the pages, a life-affirming counterpoint to the story of her death from cancer. Cartoons may seem an odd way to chronicle a couple's journey with cancer—yet in the hands of Stan Mack they are deeply moving.

A few title pages bear the names of two people linked by the word "with"—the collaboration of a nonwriter with a good story and a pro-fessional who can tell it. Stanley J. Winawer and Louise Ray Morning-star and their collaborators are two examples of such pairs.

Chapter headings and appendixes provide a frame for the stories within. Richard Galli introduces his chapters with quotes from let-ters he and his wife received during the first few weeks following his son's accident: "Please know that you are in our hearts and minds" (p. 154). Beverly Bigtree Murphy, whose husband has Alzheimer's Disease, introduces each of her chapters with lyrics from popular songs of the 1940s. Irving Berlin and George Gershwin—speaking of love that is here to stay—provide a soundtrack for her narrative. Edith Kunhardt Davis, whose son died suddenly, concludes a book-length disquisition on grief with two pages of "Books That Helped Me."

More than half the memoirs contain family pictures. Individual portraits and family scenes punctuate their pages. Culled from the family album or the dusty boxes in which they may have rested un-disturbed for years, they convey the passage of time, the mutability of meaning, what words are inadequate to express.

Phrases leap from the pages of one memoir to illuminate the meaning of another. Read one. Read many. The more you read, the more you'll see how apparent differences between this family and that, this illness and that, are but variations on a common theme—readers and writers joined in their joint humanity.

# chapter 12

## Memoirs in Brief

### "Our Inward Journey"

Jimmy Allen, *Burden of a Secret: A Story of Truth and Mercy in the Face of Aids* (Random House, 1995).

Allen could be seen as a modern-day Job—a leader of the Southern Baptist church whose faith was sorely tested by the suffering of those he held most dear. A son, daughter-in-law, and two grandchildren all had AIDS, and the religious community they had always turned to for support did not want to hear about it. As if were not enough to watch his young grandsons lose their hold on life, he also had to see the doors to normal childhood experiences closed in their faces. Averse to lying, he learned to dissemble. He found help in unexpected places. And although he emerged disillusioned with a church establishment that does not practice what it preaches, his faith in God and in the Bible's literal teaching never wavered.

Isabel Allende, *Paula* (Harper Collins, 1995).

Allende's daughter, Paula, was a young woman with plans, happy in work and fulfilled in love, when she was overtaken by a mysterious disease and fell into a coma. Through the long hours that she passed at the bedside—first in a hospital in Spain, then at their home in Chile—Allende reflected on Paula's heritage: politically prominent ancestors whose lives were inextricably bound with the history of their country. She decided to write down their stories as a gift for

Paula when she awakened. The memoir flashes back and forth in time as daily caregiving concerns alternate with tales of the past. Paula did not awaken. The rituals surrounding her death were rich in cultural symbols, seamlessly uniting both themes of this unusual memoir.

Aaron Alterra, *The Caregiver: A Life With Alzheimer's* (Steerforth Press, 1999).
In a voice that is by turns poetic and political, Alterra renders the day-to-day experience of caring for a wife with Alzheimer's Disease from the time of diagnosis (when she was driving, running a household, and rehearsing for a cello concert) to three years later (when she was wheelchair bound and unable to unclench her teeth to be fed). Whether he is describing his wife's bent yet still erotically appealing body or garnering evidence to defend his case against bureaucracies that would deny her the help she needs, his well-wrought passages echo long after the book is closed. A story of old love—the couple has been married for sixty years—this book deserves a place on the bookshelf alongside Gabriel García Márquez's *Love in the Time of Cholera*.

Martin Amis, *Experience: A Memoir* (Talk Miramax Books, 2000).
Much of this renowned British writer's memoir is devoted to the life and death of his father, the author Kingsley Amis. At the end of his life, Kingsley was an alcoholic in poor physical and mental condition. It is posited that the cause of death was Alzheimer's Disease. In his time of illness, Martin's mother returned to nurse her former husband. And when Kingsley died in a hospice, Martin and his brother chose to stay outside smoking and reminiscing while their sister sat by the bedside. The mordant wit of the author and the unorthodox behavior of the Amis family do not obscure its abiding bonds.

Barbara Lazear Ascher, *Landscape Without Gravity: A Memoir of Grief* (Penguin, 1993).
Younger brothers can be a trial to teenage sisters. They have a way of clamoring for attention, of getting in the way at just the wrong moments. And Bobby was more difficult than most. Flamboyant, over-the-top behavior marked him as different even before he came out as

a gay man interested in a theatrical career. Then the siblings grew up and went their separate ways. The distance between them was more than geographic; and although they were in touch, they did not share everything with each other—most specifically, Bobby's diagnosis of AIDS and his deteriorating health. The memoir concentrates on the period of mourning—the time when Barbara first came to know his friends, appreciate his life, and recognize all that she has missed.

Brenda Avadian, *Where's My Shoes: My Father's Walk Through Alzheimer's* (North Star Books, 1999).
When their eighty-six-year-old father began acting strangely it passed unnoticed by the son who lived with him and the daughter who lived a few blocks away. It was Brenda, the youngest, who took hold and moved him from Milwaukee to the home she and her husband shared in Los Angeles. A childless, dual-career couple who were used to being in control of their lives, they soon saw their days and nights dissolve into the chaos of caring for a physically active, cognitively impaired father. The sibling relationship strained and finally broke. Nursing home placement was soon necessary, but Brenda continued to be an active participant in her father's care. The depiction of a daughter's collaboration with the staff of a less than perfect facility rings true.

John Bayley, *Elegy for Iris* (St. Martin's Press, 1999).
——, *Iris and Her Friends: A Memoir of Memory and Desire* (Farrar, Straus and Giroux, 2000).
Iris is the esteemed British novelist and philosopher Iris Murdoch, who was diagnosed with Alzheimer's Disease—as her mother was before her—in her seventies. As unique as her gifts were, the trajectory of her cognitive decline could not have been more typical. It is the contrast with an earlier brilliance that highlights the devastation of the disease. Bayley alternates memories of their active past with vignettes from their diminished present. His reflections on the enduring nature of their bond, and conviction that Iris remains—at the essential core—the same woman he has always loved shed a unique perspective on the situation.

Martha Beck, *Expecting Adam: A True Story of Birth, Rebirth, and Everyday Magic* (New York: Berkley, 1999).

Why would a young woman on the cusp of a promising academic career undergo amniocentesis if not to terminate her pregnancy when something seriously wrong was found? So questioned Beck's colleagues, friends, and medical advisers when her unborn child was found to have Down's Syndrome. Why would she abandon all she had worked so hard for and devote herself to the care of a severely impaired child? Beck's answer will make perfect sense to some, but be incomprehensible to others. She had dreams, intuitions, visions of knowing the soul of her son before birth. In short, the pregnancy wrought a transformation in her life through which she perceived the "magic" that lies beneath the surface of daily life. The spiritual awakening that accompanies Adam's birth and early childhood casts all she had believed in a new light and infuses every aspect of his early care.

Susan Bergman, *Anonymity: The Secret Life of an American Family* (Warner Books, 1995).

If the story sounds familiar, it is probably because you've heard about this family before. Susan Bergman is the eldest of four children, the youngest of whom is the actress Anne Heche, who covered some of the same ground in her own memoir, *Call Me Crazy.* They agree on the basic facts: the church organist father who was the model of family propriety until his hidden sexual life was revealed in his illness and death from AIDS. Although the sexual secrets they tell differ (Bergman wrote only of homosexual promiscuity while Heche wrote of the sexual abuse he inflicted upon her when she was a child) they are alike in the rage that remains.

Jane Bernstein, *Loving Rachel: A Family's Journey from Grief* (Little, Brown, 1988).

Such a good baby. Only awakening from serene slumber to nurse, then back to sleep. It was so tempting to let her be. But months passed and still she did not stir—something had to be wrong. The news was all the more ominous for being vague. What was certain was an incompletely developed optic nerve and a future of severe vision impairment. What was unknown was whether the seizures and developmental delays often associated with this condition would be Rachel's fate. Watching and responding to alternately hopeful and discouraging signs exacted a toll on Rachel's parents, her older sister just entering kindergarten, and her grandparents. The memoir ends with Rachel in a specialized preschool, a future of anticipated difficulties less important than celebration of her daily progress.

Michael Berube, *Life as We Know It: A Father, a Family, and an Exceptional Child* (Vintage Books, 1998).
Michael Berube sets the first four years of his son's life against a backdrop of dazzling social analysis. Jamie was born with Down's Syndrome and a host of physical problems, but the labels used to define these become barriers in themselves. Berube considers the situation from all angles, bringing to bear the philosophies of Plato and Wittgenstein, the particulars of federal and local legislation, pedagogical philosophies of mainstreaming and inclusion, strategies of therapy, and the meaning of family. This important book challenges the social construction of what is "normal." And always there is Jamie—proudly learning to set his literal "place at the table" while readers are left to ponder his place at the metaphorical table of human society.

Greg Bottoms, *Angelhead: My Brother's Descent Into Madness* (Crown, 2000).
Spanning twenty years in the lives of two young brothers, this memoir is framed by two cataclysmic scenes. It begins with the ten-year-old author watching fourteen-year-old Michael—under the influence of LSD—have his first psychotic break. It ends with Michael serving a thirty-year sentence in the psychiatric wing of a maximum-security prison for the crime of setting fire to a house, from which his sleeping family barely escaped. Is schizophrenia or drug use enough to explain the behavior that tyrannizes the family in the years between? Or is Michael, as the author believes, basically a "vicious" personality? Either way, he is as much victim as perpetrator, and these pages tell of his hardships as well as the devastating effect his life has on the whole family.

Ianthe Brautigan, *You Can't Catch Death: A Daughter's Memoir* (St. Martin's Press, 2000).

This story of the suicide of author Richard Brautigan and all the years leading up to it is told by his only child. Throughout the period described, Brautigan's inner demons and binge drinking war with his tender protective impulses toward his daughter. The book is composed of fragments: memories, dreams, and reflections on their life together. While the details of Brautigan's life will be of particular interest to fans of his work, the enduring effects of suicide on children and grandchildren have wide resonance.

Donna L. Breen, *\*Cancer's Gift* (Rock Wren Publishing, 2000).

They were in "the bloom of familyhood," in their early thirties, raising a two-year-old daughter and a three-month-old son amid the natural beauty of Nevada. Then baby Kyle was diagnosed with neuroblastoma. Care was to be found at a teaching hospital a five-hour drive away over a mountain pass often closed with snow. Two years of treatment—agonizing tests, surgeries, and several rounds of chemotherapy—found mother and baby commuting. Weeks in the hospital's pediatric ward alternated with weeks at home. At the time the memoir was written Kyle was six years in remission and the Breens had a third child. The "gift" of the title is the gift of all she has learned of life—and love—in the wake of the experience.

Karen Brennan, *Being with Rachel: A Story of Memory and Renewal* (Norton, 2002).

Rachel was riding on the back of a motorcycle with a new boyfriend; neither of them was wearing a helmet. When the bike overturned, he received minor injuries; she was left with severe brain trauma. Brennan, a divorced woman living on her own and now enjoying her adult children as "friends," was propelled into active motherhood once more. The painstaking process of rehabilitation is described at length, as are the shifting alliances within the family. The particular challenge of caring for a brain-trauma patient is mourning the person who was and accepting the person who is. In letting go of her anger at the boyfriend and simply "being" with Rachel and in her life, Brennan survived the experience with new insight.

Patricia Broadbent and Hydeia Broadbent with Patricia
Romanowski, *You Get Past the Tears: A Memoir of Love and
Survival* (Villard, 2002).

Abandoned at birth by a drug-using mother, Hydeia tested positive
for HIV at the age of four. Fortunately, she had been adopted into
the ideal family to receive the news. The mother Patricia—a social
worker/activist for minority adoptions—was an experienced parent (there were four older children) as well as a powerful advocate.
Hydeia's charisma and Patricia's determination made for a powerful
combination. Although the next decade of Hydeia's physical care is
discussed at length, it is her public stance as a "poster child" for pediatric AIDS that is the focus of the memoir. Hydeia represents the
first generation of HIV-positive children for whom HAART (highly
active retro-viral therapy) promises a future. At the memoir's end
she is a teenager living a full life in which AIDS activism and typical
adolescent concerns seamlessly combine.

Sandy Broyard, *Standby* (Knopf, 2005).

Sandy Broyard, widow of the literary critic Anatole Broyard, wrote
this memoir six years after his death from prostrate cancer. It is reconstructed from notes made at the time events occurred as well as
from memories and updates. While some space is devoted to her
husband's last days of life and the acute period of mourning that
followed, the book concentrates on her slow coming to terms with
loss. Broyard writes of the thoughts and feelings that accompanied
the changes in her life—selling and buying a home, exchanging city
life for full-time residence by the seashore, deciding which activities
to drop, resume, or start anew. Through these everyday decisions, the
reader sees her emerging from the shadow of a paralyzing grief to a
fulfilling life alone.

Janice A. Burns, *Sarah's Song: A True Story of Love and Courage*
(Warner Books, 1995).

There was no Sarah to sing or be sung to. Sarah was the never-to-be
child of Janice and Bill Burns, who learned soon after their marriage that both were infected with HIV (the result of a brief homosexual affair he had in college). Together, they defied all recognized

stereotypes of people living with AIDS. For a white, educated, heterosexual, middle-class couple with a limitless future, the diagnosis arrived like a lightening bolt. Gone in an instant were the plans for career and a family; in its place was a struggle to resist the ravages of the disease, caring for each other, and becoming AIDS activists. The disease progressed more rapidly for Bill, who has died by the memoir's end. Although her grief was profound and her own health was frail, Janice continued to find purpose and pleasure in life.

Bebe Moore Campbell, *Sweet Summer: Growing Up with and without My Dad* (Ballantine Books, 1989).
Campbell's early life was split in many ways. Between her divorced mother and father. Between the Jim Crow laws of the South and the more subtle racial discrimination of the North. Between the urban ways of her maternal Philadelphia household, where she spent the school year, and the rural ways of her father's family in South Carolina, where she spent the sweet summers of her childhood. Between the worlds of the physically able and the disabled. Her father's college dreams for a career did not come to fruition because he was left a paraplegic after an automobile accident. Campbell never lived with her father as an adult, but frequently visited and provided physical care. This story of an African-American family on the cusp of the civil rights revolution is also a compelling story of intergenerational relationships.

Clifford Chase, *A Hurry Up Song: A Memoir of Losing My Brother* (University of Wisconsin Press, 1999).
Clifford Chase was the youngest of five children; Kevin was the next to oldest. Both were gay. They were close as children but drifted apart as adults. Kevin, HIV+, settled down in California, in the state if not the town of his childhood. Clifford, HIV-, lived across the continent in New York. He made a visit that reawakened old memories, but, as all visits do, it came to an end. Should he have returned to California to assist in the accelerating health crises or continued with his independent life, waiting for bulletins from their aging parents, who have taken over Kevin's care? Amid reports of Kevin's fluctuating condition, Clifford deliberated on the timing of his next visit.

He was still deliberating when Kevin died. Sibling relationships in a large family—and their impact in forming individual identities—are well expressed.

Susan Cheever, *Home Before Dark: A Biographical Memoir of John Cheever by His Daughter* (Houghton Mifflin, 1984).
When she learned that her father was near death, Susan Cheever began noting her experiences, thoughts, and feelings in a journal. What began as a way to help her through a difficult time evolved into a reflection on the past life of their family. A loving father who was often preoccupied, a religious man who suffered self-doubt, Cheever emerges as fully human. His last years of life were dogged by health problems: temporary memory lapses described as states of "otherness," seizures, and the cancer of which he died. This is a family of individuals whose actions often seem at cross-purposes. Nevertheless they pull together in caring for him in his last days, and in mourning his loss. A centerfold of pictures, cleverly culled from various stages and facets of John Cheever's life, adds to the narrative's power.

Ann Colin, *Willie: Raising and Loving a Child with Attention Deficit Disorder* (Penguin, 1997).
From the time of Willie's birth, his parents suspected something was wrong. Their first-born was easily distracted, hypersensitive, sometimes violent, and unable to modulate or control his behavior. As he grew, the troubling behavior escalated. He was asked to leave his first school; the second school proved barely more accommodating. A younger brother who developed normally only highlighted the problem. His parents enlisted all manner of medical professionals and social supports on Willie's behalf. The memoir (which consists of intermittent journal entries made over the first five years of Willie's life) ends on an up note. He has "graduated" from play therapy and is set to begin a private elementary school for children with special needs.

Donna Rhodes Collins, *Michael's Story: On the Wings of Love; A Grandson's Life and Death from Kawasaki's Disease* (Mayhaven Publishing, 1997).

Michael was diagnosed with Kawasaki's disease at the age of six and died at the age of sixteen. Although the intervening ten years were marked by portents of what was to come, they were lived fully. As his maternal grandmother describes all the fine traits that Michael exhibited in his too-brief life, the members of his closely knit and devoutly Catholic family are also portrayed. A minute description of important occasions in the lives of the family—punctuated by photographs and an excerpts of Michael's childhood essay on "What I am thankful for is" —forms a moving memorial. Their faith in God sorely tested by the tragedy that has befallen them, the family nevertheless finds comfort in their religious convictions and practices.

Eleanor Cooney, *Death in Slow Motion: My Mother's Descent Into Alzheimer's* (Harper Collins, 2003).

When Cooney's mother began acting strangely after the death of her beloved second husband, her physical symptoms and mental gaps were attributed to mourning and loneliness. A cross-country move—from Connecticut to Northern California—and a small home next door to her daughter did not relieve the situation. Even as her mother's mental faculties rapidly deteriorated, Cooney maintained a belief that the proper supports could restore her functioning. In rapid sequence, she moved her into her own home, hired home care, arranged an in-patient psychiatric evaluation (that subjected her mother to degradation and herself to unending guilt), and finally found an appropriate—though less than ideal—institutional care setting. Rarely is the anguish of an adult child so graphically expressed. Sorrow, anger, physical exhaustion, dependence on alcohol, an inability to fulfill her work obligations, and difficulties with her life partner all marked Cooney's care journey.

Elizabeth Cox, *Thanksgiving: An AIDS Journal* (Harper and Row, 1990).

One of the first memoirs to come out of the AIDS epidemic, this book accurately portrays the onset of medical and public awareness of what was to become a worldwide phenomenon. When AIDS entered their lives, Elizabeth and Keith were a young couple with a four-year-old son. In the beginning, the diagnosis and the knowledge of

how Keith had contracted it (an early homosexual affair) was shared
with very few people. The relationship between secrets and shame—
and its isolating effects on a family at a time when they most need
the support of community—is reflected throughout the caregiving
process, which also depicts the paucity of medical options available at
the time. More heartening are depictions of the private world the couple construct within their walls, and their efforts to provide normal
childhood experiences—particularly a bonding with his father—for
their son.

Jean Craig, *Between Hello and Goodbye: A Life-Affirming Story of
Courage in the Face of Tragedy* (Jeremy P. Taucher, Inc., 1991).
By the time Craig's husband, Kevin, died of a congenital heart condition after a thirteen-year struggle, the years of caregiving and the loss
of a beloved partner had taken their toll on her. Yet she endured: a successful advertising woman with her own business, four children now
grown, she was in no hurry to remarry. Then she met Ed—larger than
life, a healthy, hearty man who embraced her family as her own. They
traveled the world, built a home by the sea. It lasted three years, until
Ed was diagnosed with metastatic cancer. The memoir covers the year
and a half from that day to his death. Ed is a fighter who does valiant
battle until the end. From the initial diagnosis through the panoply
of treatment and surgeries to his death at the home she dubs "Cedars
Malibu"—in rueful recognition of its transformation to a hospital out-
post—the story of caring for Ed is juxtaposed with memories of caring
for Kevin. What it means to love, to care, and to lose has rarely been
as well expressed as in this wise and graceful memoir.

Edith Kunhardt Davis, *I'll Love You Forever Anyway* (Donald I.
Fine, Inc., 1995).
What could be harder to bear than the sudden death of a beloved son
at the age of twenty-seven? Perhaps only the suspicion that you were
in some way responsible. A congenitally weak heart had succumbed
before anyone had expected and, in the absence of a definitive cause,
there was blame enough to go around: Neddy, who tried to deny
his problem, the doctors who missed warning signs, and—to her
everlasting guilt—Davis herself, who was an alcoholic during her

pregnancy. Now in recovery, she faces the burden of guilt, grief, and rage. The mourning process, in all its day-to-day fluctuation of thoughts and feelings, is drawn in telling detail. An afterword, written several years after the rest of the memoir, forms a perfect coda.

Heather Choate Davis, *Baptism by Fire: The True Story of a Mother Who Finds Faith During Her Daughter's Darkest Hour* (Bantam Books, 1998).
Although Davis was baptized and confirmed in an Episcopal church, her embrace of Christianity was ambivalent. She was married by a minister who remarked on the absence of a mention of God in the ceremony she and her husband had written. She wanted her own children baptized but could not wholeheartedly enter into participation in the church congregation. Then began her trial of fire—beginning with her seven-month-old daughter's first seizure, continuing through hospitalizations, diagnostic tests, and painful treatments, and ending with successful surgery to remove a benign brain tumor. Although Davis's path to faith will be of particular interest to readers who share her religious outlook, it can resonate with others as well.

Lennard J. Davis, *My Sense of Silence: Memoirs of a Childhood with Deafness* (University of Illinois Press, 2000).
His parents were profoundly deaf. A detailed series of childhood memories (beginning with the author as an infant viewing the primal scene and ending with his admission to college) convey a single theme: Davis cried out for help and no one heard. (Few caregiving situations provide such a ready-made metaphor.) Like other children of deaf parents, he was often called upon to interpret and negotiate with the outside world. As an adult, he recalls these situations with resentment and rage. It is through involvement with CODA (Children of Deaf Adults) that Davis—who had deliberately alienated himself from Deaf culture in adulthood—begins to understand the unresolved emotions that have plagued his life.

Simone de Beauvoir, *A Very Easy Death* (Warner Books, 1973).
First published in France in 1964 under the title *Une mort tres douce*, and translated into English almost a decade later, this is one of the

earliest memoirs of family care. All of the action takes place within a four-week period in a Parisian hospital. De Beauvoir's seventy-seven-year-old mother had fallen in her apartment, was taken to the hospital with a fractured femur, and while there was diagnosed with "a huge cancerous tumor" blocking her intestine. De Beauvoir and her younger sister decided to tell their mother that the exploratory surgery revealed peritonitis from which she will recover. Reality soon intrudes as the reader keeps a bedside vigil with the author and her younger sister, spared not a detail of the pain, indignity, and suffering of the condition until the mother's final release in death. Though the narrative takes place in another country at another time, the scenes of hospital life are familiar. As might be expected, de Beauvoir's reflections on family bonds and societal forces, the mundane and the existential, add an extra dimension to the tale.

Christopher Dickey, *Summer of Deliverance: A Memoir of Father and Son* (Simon and Schuster, 1998).
A history of the intermittent, ambivalent, battered, but finally invincible relationship between the poet James Dickey and his eldest son, this memoir has at its heart the making of the film *Deliverance*, based on the novel that brought the father—already revered in literary circles—popular fame. Alcoholism is a central character here, and rarely has its imprint on the bodies of the addicted and the souls of their children been more powerfully described. By the age of eighteen, the son, believing the hero-father of his childhood responsible for his mother's alcohol-related death, had started building wedges to distance himself. He was middle-aged before he returned. With the help of his younger brother, Christopher developed and carried out an intervention that helped put a chaotic family situation to rights. It was too late for James Dickey to be restored to health but not too late for the father-son relationship to be rebuilt.

J. D. Dolan, *Phoenix: A Brother's Life* (Knopf, 2000).
Angry at the way his life had turned out, the author's adored older brother, John, had simply drifted away from the family. He had not spoken to J. D. for five years. Everyone thought there would be time for a reconciliation. Then John was caught in an explosion at a power

plant in the desert where he was working, barely surviving, third-degree thermal burns over 90 percent of his body. J. D. joined his mother and three sisters in a hospital vigil for several weeks of intensive though ultimately futile treatment. At the bedside, he called up memories of the closeness they shared in childhood and found the words to express the truth of the moment as well as of the past.

Michael Dorris, *The Broken Cord: A Family's Ongoing Struggle with Fetal Alcohol Syndrome* (Harper and Row, 1989).
This prize-winning memoir, responsible for our society's recognition of the extent and consequences of fetal alcohol syndrome—particularly in the Native American community—centers on Adam, a child he adopted at the age of three. As Dorris, a professor of anthropology at Dartmouth, slowly accepted that his son's odd behavior and cognitive deficits were innate, he embarked on a scholarly and personal quest for cause that lead him to reconsider his previous beliefs on the rights of the mother (in this case to drink during pregnancy and so irreparably damage the life of her unborn child) and become a powerful advocate for prevention. The intertwining of the personal experience of raising a disabled child (who always appears on the verge of "growing out" of his developmental delays) and the politics of public health adds to the interest of this book.

Martha Tod Dudman, *Augusta Gone: A True Story* (Simon and Schuster, 2001).
Dudman is a baby-boomer who herself experimented with drugs when she was her daughter's age. Unlike earlier caregivers who relied on established systems of psychiatric care, she and her cohorts were open to New Age approaches. When she realized that she could no longer cope with her daughter's truancy, days-long disappearances, uncontrolled furies, and heavy drug use, she turned to a network of similarly affected parents for help. Through them she learned of a boot camp, a wilderness setting in Idaho that removed troubled teens from their environment and—through a mixture of hard labor and confrontational therapy—turned them around. After a harrowing stay, Augusta returned from camp the loving, responsible daughter she once was. She found a job and had plans for the future. Dudman

ends the memoir too relieved to be skeptical, too shaken by the past to question the future.

David Eggers, *A Heartbreaking Work of Staggering Genius* (Simon and Schuster, 2000).

Coming of age stories are about young people leaving home. What happens when it is the home that leaves first? Eggers was twenty-one when (horribly and improbably) his mother and father died of cancer within five weeks of each other. He was the third of four children; the youngest, Toph, was only eight years old. The home in Lake Forest, the suburb of Chicago where they grew up, was no more. The siblings moved to California, a place of new beginnings. Always present were the underlying theme of grief and mourning, recollections of his parents' lives and deaths, and a striving to understand who, in the wake of the disaster survived, he has become. Although most of the narrative focuses on the two young brothers, the care that the older siblings provided to their parents occupies a substantial part of the book and is a particularly fine rendering of the young-adult-child as caregiver.

Brooke Ellison and Jean Ellison, *One Mother, One Daughter, One Journey* (Hyperion, 2001).

Brooke was the first ventilator-dependent person to graduate from Harvard—a feat accomplished through the constant attendance of her mother, Jean. Mother and daughter write alternating chapters of a memoir that chronicles their inseparable relationship during the years they pursued this goal. Determined that the automobile accident that paralyzed their daughter would not prevent their daughter from attending the college of her choice, Brooke's parents restructured their married and family life to make her wish come true. This is an upbeat book in which mother and daughter delight in describing the humorous incidents as well as the difficult times—yet sadness can be read between the lines. When Brooke writes of the parties she can't fully participate in, when Jean writes of preparing for her husband's weekend visit as if it were a date—the cost of the triumph is clear.

*Lon Elmer, *Why Her, Why Now: A Man's Journey Through Love and Death and Grief* (Bantam Books, 1987).
Elmer's wife was diagnosed with cancer just before their wedding, so the illness was a part of the marriage from the start. The description of their journey is stronger on Elmer's philosophy of care than on specifics of the situation or the relationship. Particularly interested in his own reactions as they unfold, Elmer deals extensively with the mourning period leading up to his re-engagement in life and search for a new partner. Some readers may view the result as solipsistic, others may appreciate the frank expression of negative and ambivalent feelings toward the patient and toward the care process that are not often expressed.

Annie Ernaux, *"I Remain in Darkness"* (Seven Stories Press, 1999).
This slim volume, translated from the French, consists of journal entries the author made during the three years that her mother suffered from Alzheimer's Disease. The writings are elliptical (they were intended for her eyes only), random ("when she was still living with me, I began jotting down on small undated scraps of paper the things she said or did that filled me with terror"), and in their original form ("echoing the bewilderment and distress that I experienced at the time"). The entries are dated by month during the early days when she tried to care for her mother at home; later, notes were written on Saturday and Sunday right after weekly visits to the geriatric-care floor of the hospital where her mother was finally placed. "I remain in darkness" is the first sentence of a letter to a friend that her mother never completed. It was the last sentence that her mother ever wrote.

Maria Flook, **My Sister Life: The Story of My Sister's Disappearance* (Pantheon Books, 1997).
Their parents had booked passage on the fatal trip of the *Andrea Doria* but changed plans before sailing. The stateroom in which Maria and Karen would have slept was occupied by two other sisters—only one of whom survived. The shipwreck is a repeated metaphor for Maria's

journey from the age of twelve (when her fourteen-year-old sister left home for a street life of prostitution and abuse) to the sister's return two years later, and the effect of this rupture on their relationship in all the years that followed. Flook recreates Karen's life during the years apart; alternating chapters written in her sister's voice with chapters written in her own; the structure, like the title, of the book reflects the author's sense of intertwined lives.

Richard Galli, *Rescuing Jeffrey* (St. Martin's Press, 2000).
The nightmare began when his teenage son, Jeffrey, dove into a swimming pool and hit his head. Wasn't it lucky that his father and some doctor friends were on hand to resuscitate him? It seemed so at the time. But when the news came that Jeffrey would be paralyzed from the neck down, Galli wondered if he had done the right thing, and seriously considered discontinuing life support. A daily journal of events—covering the period from July 5 (the day of the accident) to July 14 (when Galli decided that his son's life, however limited, was worth fighting for)—is harrowing and suspenseful. A coda, postscript, and epilogue three years later attest the wisdom of his decision. Jeffrey is a college student who is living a physically diminished but mentally and spiritually fulfilling life.

Elizabeth Glaser, *In the Absence of Angels* (Putnam, 1991).
Glaser, a speaker at the Democratic National Convention in 1992, put an unexpected face on the story of AIDS. She had received a blood transfusion following the birth of her first child and, a few years later, went on to bear a second child. There was no indication that anything was wrong until her daughter Ariel became ill at the age of six. The entire family was tested, and Glaser and both children were found to be infected with HIV. As members of their Hollywood community rallied around, the Glasers used the funds and publicity to establish a foundation for pediatric AIDS that will help thousands of children in less privileged circumstances. The private anguish of the family and the public story of their political battles intertwine in this memoir.

Mary Gordon, *The Shadow Man: A Daughter's Search for Her Father* (Vintage Books, 1996).

When Gordon became a writer, it was with the proud recognition that she was following in his footsteps of an idealized father who died when she was seven. Then she discovered unpleasant facts about his life that were far from what she imagined. She spent a year trying to reconcile her images of him and emerge with her love intact. Ironically, it is during the time that she is gaining her father that she begins to lose her mother. As depression and alcoholism slowly evolved into Alzheimer's Disease, Gordon cared for her mother at home until it became obvious that she needed a greater level of care and was admitted to a nursing home. Many themes intertwine in this memoir, resulting in a powerful narrative.

Joan Gould, *Spirals: A Woman's Journey Through Family Life* (Penguin, 1988).

At the beginning of this memoir, Gould is a wife, mother, and daughter. By its end, she is a widow, mother, and grandmother. In a scant three years, her husband and mother have died, and her daughter has given birth to a daughter. All of this makes for a dizzying shift of roles. The relationship between Gould and her mother had been dutiful rather than desired. Dependent on the care of paid attendants and a doctor who made house calls, Gould's mother was as much a captive of depression and inertia as of emphysema, heart disease, and, eventually, the succession of strokes that ended her life at the age of seventy-four. Gould envisions the journey through family life as a spiral, each rung dipping into the past even as it rises upward to the future—in a memoir in which five generations of women illustrate the imprint, as well as the possibilities of change, that form this family's legacy.

Janet Farrington Graham, *Letters to Harry: The True Story of a Daughter's Love and a Mother's Final Journey* (Time Life, 1998).

A literal faith in angels and everlasting life sustained Graham through the terminal phase of her mother's battle with breast cancer. This narrative is told in the form of letters to a colleague who is described as the author's "spiritual twin." An introduction indicates that they were all mailed on the day they were written and none were edited for this book. Although Graham is intent on conveying her religious vision, her story is typical of other tales of parent care: an unanticipated crisis (her father needs emergency angioplasty), sharing caregiving tasks with siblings, finding a balance between meeting the needs of her parents, her three young children, and herself.

Linda Grant, *Remind Me Who I Am, Again* (Granta Publications, 1998).

Long after she had forgotten who her grandson is, Grant's mother could still "match navy." Shopping continued to define who she was, even after multi-infarct dementia had destroyed her ability to remember what was said a moment before. Hers was an immigrant's England where material possessions represented escape from an Eastern European Jewish past. The story of how the Grants (formerly Ginsbergs) assimilated to Liverpool is analogous to the story of how Grant and her younger sister assimilated to the British role of "carers"—first in the community and then in a nursing home. Of particular interest in this memoir is the rare portrait of multi-infarct dementia—a disease that leaves some abilities unscathed while demolishing others.

John Gunther, \**Death Be Not Proud: A Memoir* (Harper and Row, 1949).

Continuously in print since its publication over half a century ago, this book has become a classic. The tale of a famous journalist applying his skills of gathering and integrating information to the life-and-death struggle of his only child has lost none of its narrative intensity. Johnny was a gifted Harvard-bound prep school senior when the dreaded diagnosis of leukemia is made. His divorced parents shared in the care of their only child—his treatment in hospital and at home—a process that is described in hourly detail. Although much about the treatment of cancer is different today, the family relationships and the seesaw of hope and fear are instantly recognizable.

Donald Hall, *The Best Day, the Worst Day: Life with Jane Kenyon* (Houghton Mifflin, 2005).

Jane Kenyon was a well-known poet at the time she died of leukemia at the age of forty-seven. The poems she wrote during the fifteen months she struggled with the disease bear eloquent witness to the inner state of a cancer patient. Kenyon worked until the end—creating poetry, writing her obituary, and planning her funeral. Ten years have passed. And now her husband, Donald Hall, himself a poet, looks back on their life together and his own life since her death. While this book provides an important picture of the effects of aggressive cancer treatment (bone marrow transplant) on patient and family, it is particularly strong in portraying the changing life perspective of a grieving spouse.

Molly Haskell, *Love and Other Infectious Diseases: A Memoir* (Morrow, 1990).

Haskell had so wrapped her life around her husband of twenty years (the noted film critic Andrew Sarris) that the boundaries between them blurred. The consequences of such intertwining of spirits only became evident during his months of hospitalization for a mysterious viral illness that attacked his mind as it ravaged his body: a deterioration all the more frightening for being a puzzle to the medical team. He eventually recovered. Reflections on the marital relationship—the blessings of connection and the necessity for separation—move beyond her individual experience to resonate with that of many other wives.

Joseph Heller and Speed Vogel, *No Laughing Matter* (Putnam, 1986).

The famed author of *Catch 22* was stricken with Guillain-Barre virus, and his dear friend stepped in to care for him. In alternating chapters, the two describe their experiences and emotions during the hospitalization and its immediate aftermath. The particular deficits caused by the illness and the long, difficult rehabilitative process are conveyed. Humorous set pieces (many about the romance between Heller and his nurse) and experiences with well-known personalities who are friends to both comprise most of the memoir. In fact the role of friendship—a family of choice as opposed to a family of birth or marriage—is the guiding motif of the narrative.

Julie Hilden, *The Bad Daughter: Betrayal and Confession*
(Algonquin Books of Chapel Hill, 1998).
Going away to college has a special appeal to bright and bookish adolescents who don't fit in at high school, and find no refuge at home.
The escape to a world where they can recreate themselves, free of
those who "knew them when," holds the promise of a whole new
life. For Hilden, the only child of divorced parents, the imperative
for flight was stronger than most. Her mother's drinking and erratic
behavior made for a lonely adolescence and seemed reason enough
to go away and stay away. As the years passed, news of her mother's
rapid descent into early-onset Alzheimer's Disease (she is forty-eight
at the time) reached Hilden in bulletins from a caregiving aunt. She
refused to read or keep them. The belated, final bedside visit at a time
when her mother could no longer recognize her and the mother's
death soon after are a source of enormous remorse.

Amy Hoffman, *Hospital Time* (Duke University Press, 1997).
Amy and Michael first met as colleagues working on a Boston news-
paper (*Gay Community News*) and continued their friendship after
they stopped working together. When he was diagnosed with AIDS,
she volunteered to be his primary caregiver—little anticipating what
she was letting herself in for. He was a difficult and sometimes hostile patient. His care needs were overwhelming. Buffeted by conflicting emotions—empathy, anger, exhaustion, resentment, pride—and
the concerns of her own family (what was left for them if she gave
so much of herself to friends?), she managed to fulfill her promise,
up to and including the disposition of Michael's meager belongings
after death. This is a rare memoir that limns the responsibilities and
limitations of friendship in care situations.

Tara Elgin Holley with Joe Holley, *My Mother's Keeper: A Daughter's Memoir of Growing Up in the Shadow of Schizophrenia* (Avon
Books, 1997).
Schizophrenia casts a long shadow. Holley was born to an unwed
twenty-year-old mother in the throes of her first psychotic breakdown. Until she was five, she and her mother were both cared for in

Los Angeles by her maternal grandparents. Her mother was eventually institutionalized and Holley was raised by a great aunt—coming of age just when mental hospitals began to release patients who were not a danger to themselves or others. For the next three decades, Holley struggled to create a life for herself while looking after her mother. She wavered between involvement and separation—physically and emotionally trying to find the right balance of attachment. It was with the birth of her own daughter—and the support of a husband who co-authored the book—that Holley made peace with the life she was dealt.

Ann Hood, *Do Not Go Gentle: My Search for Miracles in a Cynical Time* (Picador, 2000).
Hood does not want the reader to miss the point of her memoir. In a prologue she writes that it is the story of her "spiritual Odyssey." The inward journey described coexists with an outer journey—the search for a cure for her father, who was dying of inoperable lung cancer. Scenes of coping with the disease on the home front (where Hood and her young son lived close enough to visit her parents daily) alternate with scenes from a trip to Mexico to bring home a "miracle" and later to Europe to discover her family's roots. Hood's efforts did not prevent the inevitable. Her father's death and the memories of the family's response to the sudden death of Hood's beloved brother some years before add depth and pathos to the story.

Marsha Moraghan Jablow, *Cara: Growing with a Retarded Child* (Temple University Press, 1982).
One of the earliest first-person accounts of raising a child with Down's Syndrome, this memoir is of historical as well as human interest. At a time when little was expected of children so diagnosed, Jablow taught her daughter to read before the age of five. Cara also benefited from a host of newly developed programs—among them infant stimulation techniques. At a time when retarded children were fated for lives in institutions, this memoir painted a realistic picture of the alternative—raising them at home as an integral part of the family and the larger community.

Fenton Johnson, *Geography of the Heart* (Scribner, 1996).
Two gay men began a relationship. Larry—elegant, emotional, with
a gift for celebrating the moment—was HIV+. Fenton—reserved,
intellectual, and cautious about making a commitment—was HIV-.
Their differences did not end there. Larry was the only child of elderly Jewish holocaust survivors. Fenton was the product of a large,
rural, Christian family. Soon after they met Larry exhibited the first
symptoms of AIDS. Fenton was his caregiver through the months
that followed, until his unexpected death during a vacation trip to
Paris. The Paris experience becomes a metaphor for the relationship:
a glorious, life-changing idyll with an untimely end.

Hillary Johnson, *My Mother Dying* (St. Martin's Press, 1999).
Johnson left her Minneapolis home for college and a journalistic career, living at a distance from her mother for twenty-five years. Then
Ruth developed cancer and Johnson returned home to care for her.
The memoir is particularly good at describing the course of the illness
and the care needs engendered over the months that followed. Belatedly recognizing her mother's gifts for life and for artwork, Johnson
presents her book as a collaboration. Through the front cover illustra-
tion (showing a recent photograph of mother and daughter similarly
attired, reproductions of her mother's art, and large-type credit "Art
by Ruth Jones"), Johnson posthumously accords her mother the attention she did not offer earlier.

Rodger Kamenetz, *Terra Infirma: A Memoir of My Mother's Life
in Mine* (Schocken Books, 1985).
Believing that one must step away from a subject the better to approach it, Kamenetz uses the story of his mother's life and death
as a thread connecting a collection of observations, reminiscences,
dreams, and philosophical musings. The reader is provided with a
few grounding facts: his mother succumbed to metastasized cancer
at the age of fifty-four, leaving a husband and five children. The author was the middle child, the gifted one in whom the mother had invested the greatest hopes. Her influence on his life was a burden that
he sought to escape, and the narrative weaves back and forth with
set pieces that illustrate the pushes and pulls of that relationship.

Kamenetz's story is powerful in its rendering of the shaky ground that the premature death of a parent leaves in its wake.

Karen Karbo, *The Stuff of Life: A Daughter's Memoir* (Bloomsbury, 2003).

When her mother died of brain cancer, the author was sixteen years old. Involved in school and dates, unable to understand or express her feelings, she kept on with her life during the illness and after the death as if nothing was amiss—a strategy that was encouraged by her father, who believed that silence and a stiff upper lip were the best way to deal with life's adversity. Twenty-five years later he is recently widowed from a second marriage and suffering from terminal lung cancer, and Karbo has a chance to do for him what she didn't do for her mother. The composition of the two families involved (the author and her father each have two stepchildren and one child born to them, all of whom have a role in the care tale) adds a contemporary note to the story.

Jamaica Kincaid, *My Brother* (Farrar, Straus, and Giroux, 1997).

Kincaid fled to the States for a different life. The younger brother who remained behind in Antigua embodied the reasons why. Indolent, sexually indiscriminate, incurious about the world outside his town, he—and, in a different way, their mother, with whom he still lived—exemplified the post-colonial legacy at its worst. His diagnosis with AIDS was the occasion of increased visits and efforts to get him the best possible care—no easy task in a country with a paucity of health care services. Kincaid's reimmersion in the life of mother and brother did not erase the remembered pain, but it did lead to a reevaluation of what she had left behind and what she had incorporated within her—the solace of a garden—from the early life they shared.

Morton Kondrake, *Saving Milly: Love, Politics, and Parkinson's Disease* (PublicAffairs, 2001).

The title of this memoir accurately reflects its message. Rarely are the private and public faces of illness so intertwined. At home Kondrake was the caregiving husband of Milly—growing more frantic each day as he watched her suffer from the ravages of a degenerative disease for which there was no cure. At work, Kondrake was a television commentator with wide political access. If anyone was in a position to lobby for recognition and funds for Parkinson's Disease, it was Kondrake, and his impassioned activism drives the story. As Milly became more helpless and hopeless, his task became a race against time. Ironically, it was the diagnosis of an even greater celebrity/advocate—Michael J. Fox—that began to turn the tide. Although the memoir ends with some political gains, Milly's time was running out. This memoir is both a stirring love story and a glimpse into the inside world of political decision making.

Laura Shapiro Kramer, *Uncommon Voyage: Parenting a Special Needs Child in the World of Alternative Medicine* (Faber and Faber, 1996).

When Kramer's firstborn was diagnosed with cerebral palsy at the age of ten months, she was passively ready to accept whatever advice was forthcoming from the traditional medical establishment, but they had little to offer. Slowly she began to read, to question, and to seek out alternative forms of therapy. Osteopathy, homeopathy, body work, massage, breathing exercises, neurosensory therapy, cranial osteopathy, speech therapy, family therapy, art and music therapy—all played a role in Seth's developing functioning and kept the family on an even keel when a healthy sister was born. (A teenage Seth advances his view of the process in his own chapter.) Kramer found a new direction for her life through the care of Seth—giving up a career as a theatrical producer to become an advocate and resource for children with special needs.

Harold Kushner, *When Bad Things Happen to Good People* (Schocken, 1981; rev. ed. 2001).

The overwhelming popularity of Rabbi Kushner's slim volume took him by surprise. In his introduction to the twentieth anniversary re-edition, he recalls his original intent: to bring the wisdom of the Jewish perspective on life and death to the experience of his young son's life and death from progeria (a rare genetic condition that causes premature aging). The wide reach of his message (it has been translated into many languages and used by followers of many religions) speaks to the universality of its theme. The first word of the title—a title that has become even more widely known than the book—has frequently been misquoted, with "why" substituted for "when." Kushner's distinction between the two words is just one example of the spiritual richness to be found in a book that yields new insights at each reading.

Nathaniel Lachenmeyer, *The Outsider: A Journey Into My Father's Struggle with Madness* (Broadway Books, 2000).

Schizophrenia took its time with Charles Lachenmeyer. It allowed him to attain a Ph.D., publish two acclaimed books, begin an academic career, marry, and lovingly raise a son until the age of twelve. When he began believing that his wife and the CIA were conspiring to control his thoughts and steal his research, he left his New York home—beginning an odyssey through New England that his divorced wife and abandoned son could only trace from infrequent letters and cards. By the time his father was found dead in a rented room in Vermont, there had been no contact between them for several years. Nathaniel then began his own odyssey—tracing his father's footsteps through the years since he left. Although the author could not care for his father in life, he did so after death by bearing witness to his fight.

Martha Weinman Lear, *Heartsounds: The Story of a Love and Loss* (Simon and Schuster, 1980).

Lear's husband was a middle-aged physician, performing at top capacity in a stressful, unsatisfying job when he was stricken with the first of many heart attacks. This detailed and moving account chronicles the health rallies and setbacks that faced this childless professional couple through the few years until his death, and is particularly notable for its portrayal of the nuances of power relationships (between doctor and doctor, between doctor and patient, between husband and wife). A huge bed dominated the bedroom that the couple never got to decorate; the site of medical emergencies and marital intimacy, it serves as a powerful metaphor for the tale.

Madeleine L'Engle, *The Summer of the Great-Grandmother*
(Seabury Press, 1979).

L'Engle's narrative covers a single summer at her country home in
Connecticut, a summer in which four generations came together
under one roof: the eponymous ninety-year-old mother (who at last
year's visit was confused but still recognizably herself, but was now
in the last stages of senile dementia and unable to communicate);
fifty-two-year-old L'Engle and her husband; their teenage son; two
daughters and their husbands; and two baby granddaughters; also
a round-the-clock trio of young neighborhood women who cared
for the great-grandmother through her troubled days and inconti-
nent nights. L'Engle's philosophy of life's ultimate goodness—which
could seem treacly in less skilled hands—is persuasive. Even the
great-grandmother's death attests the rightness of things. Painless,
in her own bed, in her grandson's arms—marking his rite of passage
to manhood.

Marlys Lehmann, *All I Could Do Was Love You: The True Story
of a Daughter's Courage and a Mother's Devotion* (Adler and Adler,
1988).

Lehmann was no stranger to family tragedy. As she watched over the
recovery of her teenage daughter, Alison Diane—who was left with
multiple injuries and a leg amputation after being struck by an out-
of-control car—she thought back twenty years to the leukemia death
of a son, Andrew David, who died at the age of nine. The journal she
kept of his illness that had been put away at his death and not looked
at since is now reopened—literally and figuratively. Alison was born
two years after Andrew's death and, in Jewish tradition, was named
in his memory. The echoes of that earlier loss are heard at every stage
of Alison's recovery—adding resonance to a rehabilitation story of
surprising depth.

Gerda Lerner, *A Death of One's Own* (University of Wisconsin
Press, 1985).

They had escaped the stresses of the workaday world in New York
to an early spring vacation in the Bahamas. Suddenly, Carl's fingers

stopped obeying his commands, becoming stiffer and clumsier by the minute. It was troublesome but not yet terrifying—once home a good orthopedist would set things to rights. But it was a neurologist who was needed—the diagnosis was a brain tumor and a prognosis of months. Defying her doctor's advice, Lerner did not give up her work to become a caregiver, but this did not mean that she passed a free moment. Coordinating care, filling in the gaps, and maintaining the best of the spousal relationship while acknowledging her independent life, Lerner was aided by remembered encounters with an elderly aunt and uncle who survived the Holocaust. The parallel stories echo and rebound.

Rhoda Levin, *Heartmates: A Survival Guide for the Cardiac Spouse* (Prentice Hall, 1986).
Levin's book is a hybrid: half self-help (a guide to resources and discussion of common family dynamics), half memoir (Levin's own experience after her husband's heart attack). While the resources are outdated and much of the psychology is oversimplified, the memoir remains useful in its discussion of the effects of a young man's heart attack on his growing family.

C. S. Lewis, *A Grief Observed* (Harper, 1961).
A classic account of mourning, this slim volume has a rightful place on the required reading list of every health-care professional's study of bereavement. It is at once personal (C. S. Lewis is an English don who has lost his beloved wife to cancer not long after their marriage) and general (in its unsparing description of a spouse's feelings in the period immediately following a partner's death it is unparalleled). The author's erudition is no comfort to him in his loss, but his musings—that bear the mark of a well-furnished mind—add an intellectual depth to the raw emotion of the memoir.

Reeve Lindbergh, *No More Words: A Journal of My Mother, Anne Morrow Lindbergh* (Simon and Schuster, 2001).
Anne Morrow Lindbergh, one of the most widely known women of the twentieth century, had forgotten it all. Her husband, Charles, who

was a lightening rod for the emotions of a nation—the kidnapped and murdered child, the best-selling books, the honors—lost in a fog created by a series of strokes. Reeve was a loving daughter with the means to create an ideal home-care environment. The ravages of disease continued their relentless course until the woman renowned for her words no longer spoke, stopped eating, and died. The status of the family as cultural icons and the creativity of the caregiving effort set this story apart from other memoirs of dementia care.

Paul Linke, *Time Flies When You're Alive: A Love Story* (Birch Lane Press, 1993).

Linke's wife, Chex, was nursing their second child when she discovered a lump in her breast. Her whole life was dedicated to harmony with nature. She would not put toxic elements in her garden, so how could she put them in her body? She relied exclusively on alternative methods and went on to bear a third child though warned by a physician that carrying the baby to term would result in her death within a year after the birth. Chex proved the prediction wrong—by three days. Linke's ambivalent support of his wife's regimen and the impact of her life and death on their children and extended family is well portrayed.

Gordon Livingston, *Only Spring: On Mourning the Death of My Son; A Father's Story of a Child's Gift of Love* (Marlowe and Company, 1995, 1999).

Livingston might have titled his book *On Mourning the Death of My Sons*. But who could bear to pick up a book that he could scarcely survive to write? In little more than a year this psychiatrist/father of six lost his oldest child, Andrew (age twenty-two), to suicide and his youngest child, Lucas (age six), to leukemia. The memoir is constructed around journal entries from the December to May struggle of a bereft father to live with what he calls the "randomness" of life, as well as his own actions. The impact of a child's death on family in all of its forms (nuclear, step, extended) is one of the many themes that emerge from this memoir—not the least of which is the spiritual seeking of a religious man who, in mid-life, is first questioning the beliefs on which his life has been predicated.

Doris Lund, *Eric (Harper and Row, 1974, 1989).
Her teenage son had been diagnosed with leukemia and Lund was determined that he experience all of life he could before his untimely death. She maintained this philosophy through repeated hospitalizations and homecomings, through the agonizing treatments and the treasured plateaus. In letting go of her desire to protect him (from the possibility of infection, from the disappointments of misplaced affection), her decision to let him run free was difficult but ultimately justified. Eric died as a man—taking risks, and finding the love of his life. An introduction to the second edition tells of the consequences of Eric's life and death fifteen years later.

Jackie Lyden, *Daughter of the Queen of Sheba* (Penguin, 1997).
Lyden was twelve years old when her mother first appeared garbed as the Queen of Sheba, bequeathing to each of her three daughters a country. Jackie, the eldest, received Mesopotamia—and a future of care for a parent whose colorful forays into the world of fantasy were simultaneously humorous and terrifying. Increasingly frequent episodes that escalated from an abundance of creative energies to out-of-control behavior were the key manifestations of what was ultimately diagnosed as manic-depressive illness. The effect of a mother's mental illness on each of her children is a subtext of this memoir. Although Lyden's mother was finally stabilized on Lithium, the consequences of her years of madness are writ clear in all that she and her daughters have become.

Stan Mack, *Janet and Me: An Illustrated Story of Love and Loss* (Simon and Schuster, 2004).
The story of breast cancer . . . in cartoons? Any doubts one might have about the medium suiting the message are quickly put to rest through Stan Mack's rendering of the experience shared with his life partner of eighteen years. In fact, the line drawings that illustrate monologues and dialogues are more expressive than any text markings could be. Taken together with conventional paragraphs by the author and reproduced letters by Janet, the humor and horror of daily life for a couple facing cancer together is eloquently portrayed.

Andrew H. Malcolm, *Someday: The Story of a Mother and Her Son* (Knopf, 1991).
This memoir asks a single question: "When don't we do what we can do?" when it comes to life-prolonging technology. As a journalist, the middle-aged author has interviewed and written about families who chose to "pull the plug" and physicians who supported them. As the only child of a seventy-five-year-old mother who has no chance for any quality of life if she is disconnected from the machines that sustain her, he confronted the dilemma himself. Since this book was written, "advanced directives" are recognized in most states and health care proxies are increasingly a part of the admission packet to hospitals. But the essential question—what is "natural" in life and death?—remains.

Greg Manning, *Love, Greg and Lauren* (Bantam Books, 2002).
Lauren barely survived the September 11 attack at the World Trade Center. Burns covered over 80 percent of her body, and it was doubtful if she would recover at all, much less reclaim her former life. In response to the large network of relatives and friends seeking updates on her condition, her husband Greg began to send daily e-mails. These continued for the next three months, eventually turning into a diary of their lives. He signed each entry with both their names "as a token of faith in her." By the book's end, Lauren is able to write her own message. Although the circumstances under which Lauren was injured are historic and unique, the long, difficult rehabilitation of a burn victim and its consequences for the family are not. As Lauren painfully passed one challenge after another, Greg struggled to continue working and—with the help of grandparents who move in for the duration—caring for their young child.

Jane T. McDonnell, *Notes from the Border: A Mother's Memoir of Her Autistic Son* (Ticknor and Fields, 1993).
Each member of what could easily be labeled a "dysfunctional" family was wounded in a different way, yet this is an engaging and optimistic book. Amid the turmoil in the household—the rages and recriminations, the schools and treatment centers, the professional therapists

and self-help groups—their unique strengths shine through. The story—of the birth to young adulthood world of a "high-functioning autistic" son, a daughter who disproved early diagnoses of disability, and an academic couple whose commitment to literature and teaching is both a buffer and a stress—is rendered in intense, absorbing detail. An afterword by the son, providing his view of the events described by his mother, adds to the kaleidoscopic beauty of the book.

Teresa Rhodes McGee, *Jim's Last Summer: Lessons on Living from a Dying Priest* (Maryknoll, N.Y.: Orbis Books, 2002).

Teresa McGee was a colleague who admired Jim Lenihan's professional work although she knew little of his personal life. When Jim—a seventy-year-old priest, a recovering alcoholic, and a former missionary in Africa—was dying of terminal cancer in a hospice, he asked her help in constructing his autobiography. Teresa was a young mother suffering from rheumatoid arthritis and depression. In Jim's acceptance of his disease, his ability to fully live each day and trust in God's will, she found a lesson for herself. The interweaving of their two stories escapes what could be a tractlike sermon to become a skillful and moving narrative.

George McGovern, *Terry: My Daughter's Life-and-Death Struggle with Alcoholism* (Villard, 1996).

When the forty-five-year-old daughter of a former senator and presidential candidate freezes to death in an alcoholic stupor, it is impossible not to wonder: where was her family? In this memoir, her father answers this question. As a child, Terry showed all the promise of her four siblings. Yet they successfully navigated the terrain of adolescence to reach adulthood. She did not. For twenty-five years she waged an eventually losing battle against depression and alcoholism. Following conflicting professional advice, McGovern and his wife alternated between minimum and maximum involvement in Terry's life. This memoir is a father's late-night argument with himself. With devastating honesty, he wavers between self-blame and forgiveness, between agonizing that he could have done more and recognizing all that was beyond his control.

Sue Miller, *The Story of My Father* (Knopf, 2003).
For those who work with demented elders, the progression of Miller's father through the stages of Alzheimer's Disease, his care needs and treatment, and the effect on his adult children could not be more typical. For his daughter, a prolific novelist, it is a story so rare and puzzling that it takes three tries over the period of a decade for her to come to grips with it. The dawning awareness of the author that this is not his story, but hers, and the meaning that she takes from its writing embody the special gift of this book.

Kate Millett, *Mother Millett* (Verso, 2001).
Kate Millett knew that the personal is political. As a key theorist of the woman's movement she had bared her own life in print—and worried about how the espousal of feminist and lesbian concerns would affect her mother in St. Paul. She had underestimated that woman's ability to change her ideas with the times and the unconditional love she had for a daughter who dared to risk. Now her mother had cancer, and her deteriorating condition required that her daughter relinquish all personal and professional activities in the East and move in to provide care. Applying the same analytic and advocacy perspective to the health-care system as she had to the patriarchal system, Millett adds an important dimension to the story of parent care.

Paul Monette, *\*Borrowed Time: An AIDS Memoir* (Harcourt, Brace, Jovanovich, 1987).
Widely reviewed and lauded at the time of its publication, this memoir was the first exposure that many readers had to a gay relationship or to HIV/AIDS. Roger was an attorney and Paul was a writer. Both were infected with the virus, but it was Roger who first fell ill and Paul who cared for him. Memories of their long past together—a rich tapestry of shared joys—punctuate their journey from diagnosis to death. The couple were blessed in many ways: accepting parents, devoted friends, and the best care available at the time. Yet they battled with the prejudices surrounding the disease as surely as they did its symptoms. Monette's description of his partner's life and death with

AIDS was powerful in 1987. Now it stands as a testament to gay life as it was in that time.

Margaret Moorman, *My Sister's Keeper* (Norton, 1992).
Two southern sisters of genteel upbringing: Sally, the elder (diagnosed in adolescence with schizophrenia, rediagnosed a decade later with manic depression), stayed on in the old hometown, marginally functional and under the protective eye of their widowed mother; and Margaret, the younger, moved away to find love and work in New York City. When the mother suddenly died, Margaret was forced to take hold of the situation and in the process found a peace of mind and self-knowledge that had formerly eluded her. Sally settled down—age, improved medications, and paid care-managers all play a role—and the sisters discovered how much they meant to each other. Although Sally's basic goodness and Margaret's organizational skills combine for a happy ending, the pain both endured along the way is not sugarcoated. This memoir is an especially good treatment of long-distance care.

Louise Ray Morningstar with Alexia Dorsznski, *Journey Through Brain Trauma: A Mother's Story of Her Daughter's Recovery* (Dallas, Tex.: Taylor Publishing, 1997).
When her seventeen-year-old daughter, Misti, sustained brain trauma and other serious injuries in an automobile accident, Morningstar became her constant companion. During the year-long in-patient and out-patient rehabilitation process, she put her own life on hold. Although Misti eventually recovered many of her abilities, violent rages, sexual acting out, inappropriate conversation, and short-term memory lapses persisted. And, in a final irony, mental health professionals blamed Misti's emotional problems on her being too "enmeshed" with her mother. Helpers were brought in to provide socialization and supervision. The graceful Misti, who had danced so beautifully, now awkwardly loped about. The academically gifted Misti, who was bound for Harvard and a career as a physician, now struggled with community college. Yet by the story's end Misti has graduated and married. And Morningstar has returned the life she knew before.

Beverly Bigtree Murphy, *He Used to Be Somebody: A Journey
Through Alzheimer's Disease Through the Eyes of a Caregiver*
(Boulder, Colo.: Gibbs Associates, 1993).

It was the second marriage for both. The groom was already experiencing lapses—brief episodes of memory loss and confusion,
illegible handwriting, and a mysterious sight problem that could neither be diagnosed nor corrected. Still, it didn't make sense to wait.
Beverly felt lucky to have found Tom and sure that they could weather
whatever the future held. The following decade is chronicled in detail. As Tom's abilities steadily crumbled under the onslaught of Alzheimer's, so did the supports she had relied upon. She gave up her
work to care for him. Money was tight. She became ill herself. Enduring love, belief in the power of positive thinking, and her past work as
a rehabilitation counselor served Beverly in good stead. Through the
Alzheimer's Association she became a speaker and social activist; in
helping others she helped herself.

Jay Neugeboren, *Imagining Robert: My Brother, Madness, and
Survival* (Henry Holt and Company, 1997).

They grew up as close as two brothers could be. Children of an un-
happily married, working-class couple in Brooklyn, they shared a
bedroom, keen intelligence, wide-ranging curiosity about the world,
and a potentially promising future. But Robert succumbed to mental
illness in adolescence and—despite brief periods of remission and
community living—spent most of his life indifferently cared for in
a variety of institutions. The decades that spanned Robert's illness
were marked by changing theories and treatments for mental illness,
which Jay meticulously describes. Although Jay married and had a
family as well as an academic and literary career, he too seemed captive to the illness. As he chronicles the ups and downs of his brother's
life, it is clear that his own life is irrevocably marked.

Sherwin B. Nuland, *Lost in America: A Journey with My Father*
(Knopf, 2003).

The acclaimed physician/author of *How We Die* and other narratives
of the illness experience of patients has his own story to tell. Beginning with the paralyzing depression that afflicted him in middle age,

backtracking to his childhood within an extended immigrant family in the Bronx, and fast-forwarding to his present as a man at peace with himself, Nuland views his family story as emblematic of larger social issues. The father whose moodiness, halting gait, and incontinence once angered and embarrassed him is now seen as the victim of a devaluing society and a devastating disease (syphilis caused neurological damage), and the strengths he showed in getting through each day are newly appreciated. Nuland, who felt guilty for succeeding in the land where his father had failed, now sees himself as carrying on the family legacy.

Kenzaburo Oë, *A Healing Family* (Tokyo: Kodansha International, 1996).
Kenzaburo Oë is a Nobel Laureate in literature whose life and work were profoundly influenced by an eldest son who was born with severe brain damage. Hikari had such a poor prognosis at birth that his father hesitated over authorizing life-saving surgery. It was finally performed and the son grew into adulthood—autistic, with limited speech, awkward gait, and debilitating seizures, but possessing a beauty of spirit that revealed itself through gifted musical composition. Written over a period of years, these entries explore the impact of Hikari's life on the entire family. As he came to understand Hikari's world, Oë learned more about himself. Through caring for Hikari, the couple and their younger son and daughter learned a "patience" that served them well in dealing with all of life.

Clara Claiborne Park, *The First Eight Years of an Autistic Child, with an Epilogue Fifteen Years After* (Little, Brown 1967, 1982).
————, *Exiting Nirvana: A Daughter's Life with Autism* (Little, Brown, 2001).
Why wrest your child from the tranquility of a self-created nirvana and force her to confront the stresses of an unpredictable, frightening world? And keep at it, year after year—tirelessly devising new strategies, meticulously chronicling each advance and setback? For this mother, the answer was simple: To be human is to share in the exhilarating and sorrowful experiences of life. Jessy had a right to the human condition. Park's books have become classics, providing

an overview of professional and lay thinking about autism that spans forty years. Beginning in the 1960s (when rejecting mothers were seen as the cause of autism, and expectations for diagnosed children was low) and continuing to the 1990s (when Jessy is working in a university mailroom, helping with household chores, and producing acclaimed artwork), the book portrays a long, hard journey. Facing a future in which she and her husband will be gone and Jessy must count on the support of others—particularly her three older siblings—is not a fear for Park. She trusts in a "future (she) cannot see" and after two volumes of this rich family saga, the reader does too.

Ann Patchett, *Truth and Beauty: A Friendship* (HarperCollins, 2004).

This story chronicles the friendship between two writers who are as different in temperament and life situation as they are bound in literary tastes and mutual dependence. Lucy Grealy suffers from the aftereffects of treatment for childhood cancer, including blows to her self-esteem arising from profound facial disfigurement, and difficulty eating and sleeping due to constant pain and the cumulative effect of thirty-eight unsuccessful surgeries. Her fragile physical and emotional health make her a ripe target for abuse of prescription drugs and eventually heroin. Patchett carries Grealy—physically and emotionally—through the crises that arise at every turn. Ironically, the overdose that took Grealy's life happened during one of the few times when Patchett was not available.

Charles P. Pierce, *Hard to Forget: An Alzheimer's Story* (Random House, 2000).

Small wonder that Pierce obsessively tried to recall trivia, gazed into the faces of his sleeping children to wonder which of his genes lived on in them, and set himself the task of researching all that is known about the "family disease" that has become the "family curse." Pierce's father and all four of his father's siblings were afflicted with Alzheimer's in their late sixties to early seventies. This story is told through parallel themes: the scientific race to discover the cause of Alzheimer's and the family's struggle to care for Pierce's father. Pierce's wife was the primary caregiver—valiantly trying to raise their children while maintaining dignity and some quality of life for her rapidly deteriorating father-in-law and angry and neglectful mother-in-law. After five years, the father finally entered a home and did well until his death about a year later. And his mother thrived in the remaining years of her life. This is an essential book that is both educative and moving.

Janet Reibstein, *Staying Alive: A Family Memoir* (Bloomsbury, 2002).

When a healthy woman in the prime of life considers prophylactic mastectomy, her odds of getting breast cancer must be great. So it was with Reibstein, whose mother and two maternal aunts suffered and died of the disease. In addition to telling Reibstein's own story, this memoir details the illness and death experiences of these women. They were unfortunate enough to develop the disease at a time when disfiguring radical mastectomies were the norm, when breast cancer patients suffered isolation, shame, and stigma in addition to the ravages of the disease, when public awareness was nil and there were no support systems or services to buffer the impact. Up-to-date technology and attitudes notwithstanding, Reibstein has her own struggles in accepting the surgery, which ultimately proves to have been wise (precursors of the disease are found). This book is an important historical document as well as a compelling personal history of family care.

Joan L. Richards, *Angles of Reflection: Logic and a Mother's Love* (W. H. Freeman, 2000).

A professor of the history of science with a scholarly interest in the work of DeMorgan (a Victorian mathematician who pioneered probability theory), Richards was getting ready for a sabbatical year in Germany when her nine-year-old son required brain surgery. The surgery was successful, but his health problems continued abroad and her struggles to obtain health care for him while fulfilling her research agenda made for a fascinating juxtaposition. Searching through DeMorgan's writings, she discovered that the illness and death of his beloved daughter influenced his work and realized that the academic book she planned to write during her year abroad would not be complete without her personal story. The philosophical implications of mathematics and physics—what is necessary, what is contingent—have never been more clearly conveyed than in this multilayered narrative.

Marion Roach, *Another Name for Madness* (Houghton Mifflin, 1985).

Just out of college, Marion and her older sister, Margaret, were in their late father's journalistic footsteps—reveling in their entry-level editorial jobs at the *New York Times*. When their active, vibrant mother starts forgetting things soon after her fiftieth birthday, they attributed it to menopause. But the symptoms accelerated and became more bizarre, and within a few years they had to accept the diagnosis of Alzheimer's Disease. This memoir chronicles their search for aid—a search especially moving because they themselves were so young, without any older family members to turn to, and dealing with a situation not as well understood at the time as it is today. A variety of care situations were tried before they regretfully admitted her to a nursing home, where she adjusted rapidly. Of greatest interest in this memoir is the relationship between the sisters.

Betty Rollin, *Last Wish* (Simon and Schuster, 1985).

The last wish of Rollin's widowed seventy-six-year-old mother was "for it to be over." In the two years since being operated on for metastatic ovarian cancer she has enjoyed an eight-month remission framed by two devastating courses of chemotherapy. After ascertaining that this was not a wish of the moment but a legitimate exercise of self-determination, Rollin and her husband decided to help her mother die. Their search for a method ended in many closed doors until they finally made phone contact with a physician in Amsterdam, who advised them on the pills that would be most effective. The legal and emotional aftermath of the act on Rollin and her husband begs for further commentary. Since this memoir was written, hospice care is more widely available and palliative measures in greater use. Nevertheless, the issue of assisted suicide remains very much with us.

Nancy Rossi, *From This Day Forward: A True Love Story* (Times
Books, 1983).

The Rossis were a young married couple with a rosy future. He
was bound for a partnership in a prestigious New York City law
firm. She was pregnant with their first child. He suddenly developed a virulent case of cancer—brought on by asbestos exposure
during a brief summer job—and died just before she gave birth. As
mother-to-be and primary caregiver, Rossi's situation was physically
and emotionally draining. As new mother and widow, it was even
more so. She discovered strengths within herself that she never
knew existed. Collecting memories of her late husband to pass on
to their son, while envisioning a future life for herself, she found
the strength to move on.

Philip Roth, *Patrimony* (Simon and Schuster, 1991).

Anyone familiar with Roth's fiction will recognize this father and son.
The irrepressible champion of Newark, American, Jewish, and family history—with fixed opinions about everyone and everything—was
now a widowed eighty-six-year-old. His admiring son was helping
him make his way through a suddenly changed universe where the
only thing fixed is man's mortality. After a brain tumor is diagnosed,
his condition deteriorated and he was soon at home with a full-time
housekeeper, barely able to function physically, but retaining an active
interest in life until the end. Facing his father's death, Roth mused
about which of his father's personal possessions would constitute
his legacy. In the end, it was not the shaving mug or anything else
tangible that was his patrimony, but the memory of an intimate act
of hands-on care.

Ron Rozelle, *Into That Good Night* (Farrar, Straus, and Giroux,
1998).

It is painful to see the abilities of a once-powerful parent diminished
by Alzheimer's Disease—all the more so when that parent is as com-
manding a presence as Rozelle's father. It had taken an autocratic
and self-assured superintendent to face down the opposition and ra-
cially integrate the public schools in his small East Texas town in the

1960s. As he cared for his father, Rozelle recalled his own defining experience—military service in Vietnam. The juxtaposition of personal lives with the political Zeitgeist of a place and time enriches this detailed and loving memoir of parent care.

Diane Rubin, *Caring: A Daughter's Story* (Holt, Rinehart, and Winston, 1983).

Although her parents were still relatively young—her mother was sixty-seven, her father was seventy-two—they have had a variety of health problems over the years and it was expected that Rubin would be available to help. On the day Rubin's mother began chemotherapy for breast cancer and her father had a stroke less than twelve hours later, she embarked on a care journey that lasted until the mother's death three years later. This memoir consists of recollections interspersed with journal entries made at the time. This is a family where emotions are freely and loudly expressed. (It is also the rare memoir in which family therapy is featured.) Rubin alternately chastises and forgives herself and others in this authentic family portrait—a humorous, clamorous clan under duress.

Lillian B. Rubin, *Daughters, Mothers, and the Crucible of Aging* (Beacon, 2000).

Now a psychoanalyst in her seventies, Rubin has spent a professional lifetime studying the mother-daughter bond and a personal lifetime trying to undo the aftereffects of being raised by a depressed and rejecting mother. Through the years, she had been successful in keeping a continent between herself and her mother as well as raising her own daughter in a very different way. So why—especially given the fact that she's not in the best of health herself—did Rubin feel compelled to fly cross-country to visit her mother in a nursing home? Filled with self-questioning and informed by psychoanalytic theory that links her personal experience with that of many other mothers and daughters, this book is a valuable addition to the literature.

LeAnne Schreiber, *Midstream: The Story of a Mother's Death and a Daughter's Renewal* (Penguin, 1990).

Schreiber had decided to give up her prestigious editorial job in New York City and buy a country home in the Catskills. There she would indulge her love of nature, fishing, reading, and writing—living to her own rhythms at last. Schreiber was arranging for her move when she learned that her seventy-five-year-old mother in Minneapolis had just been diagnosed with pancreatic cancer, with "two to six months to live." The daily journal covers the following year, primarily the nine remaining months of her mother's life. The daily reality of cancer care is concretely portrayed here, as is the isolation of seemingly connected family members. The book's epilogue a year and a half after her mother has died reveals that her father is dating. Life goes on. The theme of renewal—the renewal after a great grief, the renewal of the natural world—connects all the strands of this memoir.

Alan Shapiro, *Vigil* (University of Chicago Press, 1997).

Beth was in a hospice dying of cancer and—for the last four weeks of her life—her parents and brothers joined her husband and young daughter in the vigil. Relations among them had always been rocky, and this unanticipated tragedy highlighted the problems. Beth's liberal political views and inter-racial marriage distanced her new family from her old. So the grief of the present moment is superimposed upon a tangled web of past emotions. The slow reconciliation of the two parts of Beth's life is bittersweet with regret over the years of lost time. Alan, her brother, has always been the closest to Beth and her husband. Now, as he sits by her bedside each day noting the changes in her condition, and doing what he can to help ease her death, he reflects on their shared past as well as the sad state of cancer care—even in a supposedly supportive facility.

Dani Shapiro, *Slow Motion: A Memoir of a Life Rescued by Tragedy* (Random House, 1998).

At the age of twenty-three, Shapiro was on a self-destructive path. She had abandoned the practices of her Orthodox Jewish home and

dropped out of college at the age of twenty to be a sometime ac-
tress/model and a full-time mistress to a rich, famous, married man
twice her age. The luxurious life and addictions to alcohol and co-
caine lulled her into a state of numbness that was only penetrated
by the news that her parents had barely survived a car crash. At the
hospital she found that her father has sustained brain damage; he
was to die within weeks. Her mother's survival was questionable;
she ultimately regained full functioning. The accident—and the care
experience that follows—marked a turning point in the author's life.
She broke off the relationship with her lover, entered AA, returned
to college, completed graduate school, and signed the contract for
her first book.

T. M. Shine, *Fathers Aren't Supposed to Die: Five Brothers Reunite
to Say Good-Bye* (Simon and Schuster, 2000).

This memoir is about the expected and unexpected ways men
meet death. The book jacket features the text of a living will, on
which the book's title is superimposed; the document serves as a
centerpiece around which the narrative revolves. The middle-aged
brothers (estranged by the drift of separate lives rather than any
falling out) come together at the hospital bedside of their father,
who has been comatose since his latest brain surgery. In the succeeding weeks, during which they become "hospital rats"—spelling
each other through a vigil that is marked by contradictory medical opinions on the wisdom of prolonging their father's life—they
reminisce on a shared childhood and accept their adult differences.
Hours before the father dies, one of the brother falls and suffers
a fatal concussion. At its conclusion, the author reflects that they
were all close at the beginning and at the end and regrets the time
lost in the middle.

Alex Kates Shulman, *The Good Enough Daughter* (Schocken
Books, 1999).

As the title suggests, this memoir is about Shulman's debate with
herself and the conclusion she eventually reaches. Whether or not
the reader agrees with her judgment, the story of a decades-long
separation and eventual reunion is compelling. Shulman reentered

her parents' life after the death of her fifty-eight-year-old adopted brother; a year older than she, he had remained in Cleveland and so assumed primary responsibility for their parents. Now reunited, Shulman is in constant contact—phoning daily and flying in frequently from her home in New York to arrange care. Although they had been independent until well into their eighties, her mother now has Alzheimer's Disease and her father is frail from a weak heart and frequent falls. After their admission to a multilevel geriatric facility, Shulman stays in the large house by herself during these visits and, in the process of closing it up and preparing it for sale, discovers the papers and photos that help her reclaim their lives—the outcome of Shulman's journey home.

Rachel Simon, *Riding the Bus with My Sister* (Houghton Mifflin, 2000).

Two sisters rode together on a bus. Rachel was a bright, independent, physically fit woman with a demanding professional career; Beth was a mentally retarded, obese woman who lived in a protected housing complex for the disabled. Who had the more fulfilling life? It was Beth, who, despite what others would see as insurmountable obstacles, had found love to fill her nights (a young man with similar problems) and "work" to fill her days (riding from one end of the line to another on the various buses in her county in Pennsylvania, forming personal relationships with the drivers, and becoming something of a legend in her town). Rachel decided to accompany her sister on these rides for a year. In the process she learned something about herself and about life that allowed her to overcome her fear of commitment and reconnect with a beloved man she had once rejected. A complicated and difficult childhood binds the two sisters as surely as their current companionship—making for an unusual and suspenseful book.

Bob Smith, *Hamlet's Dresser* (Scribner, 2002).

Smith was only ten when a librarian gave him a copy of *The Merchant of Venice* and he read the line "In sooth I know not why I am so sad." Shakespeare saved his life. At home was a severely retarded younger sister, Carolyn, a distant father, and a mother who was unable to cope without the help of her young son. A damaged beginning cast a shadow over Smith's life. Yet words proved redemptive. From his years as a dramatic coach to the teaching of Shakespeare to elderly people in senior centers, Smith used all that he had seen and been. Studded with quotes from Shakespeare and impressions of legendary actors he has known, anchored by a voice that is both pained and joyful, this is a beautiful book.

Ted Solotaroff, *Truth Comes in Blows* (Norton, 1998).
Although he lived a half-hour away, Solotaroff only saw his father "every year or two"—an estrangement begun when he went away to college and maintained throughout his adult life. The physical and emotional abuse in his childhood home seemed ample justification for maintaining his distance. The eldest of three children and champion of their downtrodden and eventually divorced mother, he absorbed the brunt of his father's wrath. Yet when his father began to fail, Solotaroff answered the call. The father suffered from poor circulation and arthritis and depression. For the next two years, Solotaroff and his wife did what they could to ease the last years of an alternately cantankerous and pitiful old man. In the course of their meetings, father and son talked together as they never had before, and Solotaroff learned for the first time of his father's brutal childhood and came to a new understanding of a vulnerability long concealed.

Danielle Steele, *His Bright Light: The Story of Nick Traina*
(Random House, 1998).
In many ways, Steele's life resembled that of the heroines of her best-selling romance novels: a glamorous world of luxury and travel, access to the best of everything, and a "money is no object" approach to all of life's pleasures and trials. And she met the mental illness (manic depression) and drug addiction of her first-born son, Nick, with every personal and financial resource available. She supported him through a difficult late adolescence and into a career as a rock musician. Unfortunately, it was not enough to save him and he committed suicide at the home of a caregiver with whom she was doing "tag-team" mothering. In hopes that her story of what went right—

and wrong—in Nick's life will help others avoid such a tragic end, she wrote this book and set up a foundation in his name.

Maggie Strong, *Mainstay* (Little Brown, 1988).
It was Strong who coined the term "well spouse," and this book became the rallying point for a national network of husbands and wives. Multiple sclerosis—a chronic, slowly progressive disease—is usually diagnosed in early adulthood. Strong's husband was the father of two young children when he was stricken; and this story is about the changing dynamics of his family over the years. It is particularly good in discussing children's responses to a disabled parent. Each chapter of this personal story alternates with a chapter of expert opinion about coping with chronic illness in the family. There is also a resource guide. Although much of the statistical and contact information is outdated, the issues addressed are enduring.

Elizabeth Swados, *The Four of Us* (Farrar, Straus, and Giroux, 1991).
Swados is best known as a composer, and this memoir has the structure of a theme and variations. Each section is centered on one member of her family: a schizophrenic older brother, a depressed and ultimately suicidal mother, an angry and overwhelmed father, and herself. Many of the same family stories appear in each section, but the changed context and perspective give them added resonance. The emotional cost of family secrets is the subtext of this memoir. Swados alternated between flight and return as she despaired and tried to extract the goodness of her heritage while protecting herself from its destructive pull.

Calvin Trillin, *Messages from My Father* (Farrar, Straus, and Giroux, 1996).
This memoir is a tribute to the memory of Trillin's father and an idyllic childhood in Kansas City. The father had a severe heart attack at the age of forty-nine, and was "frail" for the next decade, until his death at the age of sixty. When Trillin received the message to call home while on a trip to Kenya, his first thought was that his father had

died. The fact that he was so far away reads as strangely fitting. The father's expectation for him was to go out and live life. His mother and sister were expected to be caregivers, as one assumes they were. And as the father might have planned, it is the son who preserved the family legacy—of hard work, folk wisdom, and humor—and shares it with the world.

Calvin Trillin, *Remembering Denny* (Warner Books, 1993).
In the 1950 s Yale University was primarily an enclave of the privately educated upper classes. Trillin and Denny shared a middle-class public school upbringing that marked them as outsiders. Denny was golden boy whose athletic and academic prowess marked him as bound for success; he was the envy of classmates and parents at graduation—only to fall from sight soon after. Decades later, when the news of Denny's suicide reached him, Trillin set himself the task of remembering what he could of the old days as well as finding out what had happened to Denny since then. This memoir is not a detective story. Trillin can only surmise what stifled Denny's early promise. And it is not a family-care narrative. The author was neither related to Denny nor involved in his adult life. Nevertheless, it earns its place in this collection because of a form of caring that is significant on its own terms: the tribute Trillin pays to the memory of a friend.

Gloria Vanderbilt, *A Mother's Story* (Knopf, 1996).
Gloria Vanderbilt was used to having her private suffering treated as public property. But nothing could have prepared her for the media blitz that followed her teenage son's jump from the terrace of their New York City apartment—or the generally accepted belief that it was a planned suicide. Maintaining that it was an accident, a sleepwalking incident brought on by prescribed medication, Vanderbilt stressed all the facts of his individual and family life that bolster her position. With time and the support of good friends, Vanderbilt slowly gained the strength to face life after her devastating loss.

Abraham Verghese, *The Tennis Partner* (HarperCollins, 1998).
Verghese and David Smith crossed paths at a significant time in both their lives. Both were transplants from other countries and physi-

cians at the same hospital in El Paso, Texas. Verghese was new to the community and going through a divorce. Smith had an equally uncertain home life and had just returned to work after completing a rehabilitation program for drug-addicted doctors. Tennis became a shared recreation and passion—a place to dissolve the tension of their lives. Verghese did not immediately recognize his friend's relapse into drug use, and when he did it was too late. David Smith died of an overdose, much to the sorrow of all who mourned his untimely end.

Lou Ann Walker, *A Loss for Words: The Story of Deafness in a Family* (Harper and Row, 1986).

"Be good" meant more in Walker's family than it did in most. The eldest of three hearing daughters of profoundly deaf parents, she was entrusted with adult responsibilities while still a child. It was not that her parents wish to burden her—they were as independent as they could be—but her ability to communicate with the outside world was too crucial to the family's well-being to lie untapped. After high school, Walker left the Indiana landscape of her family, moving first to Harvard, then to New York City and life as a magazine editor. It was then that she found herself obsessively moonlighting as a sign language interpreter and teaching sign language—and began to wonder what blend of guilt and longing was goading her on. The characters in this memoir are beautifully drawn, especially the diffidence and dignity of Walker's mother and father. As adults the three daughters spoke together for the first time, of the irremediable losses and special gifts of growing up in this insular family.

Mary-Lou Weisman, *Intensive Care: A Family Love Story* (Random House, 1982).

Peter was four years old when he was diagnosed with muscular dystrophy, a fatal degenerative disease from which he would die while still in his teens. In the meantime he had a life to live—a life that his parents dedicated themselves to making as normal as possible. There were many heartaches along the way. Watching a son who was two years younger develop and outpace a declining Peter. The termination of a pregnancy when it is learned that the fetus is a boy and also at risk for the genetic disease. Frequent and frightening hospital episodes. The parents picked up stakes and moved first to California, then to England in the search for alternative approaches—to no avail. Yet the book is not unremitting tragedy; it is witty, life-affirming confirmation of the importance of living each day to its fullest.

Richard Wertime, *Citadel on the Mountain: A Memoir of a Father and Son* (Farrar, Straus, and Giroux, 2000).

Wertime's father was a curious blend of brilliance and madness, kindness and cruelty. One moment he was helping his adult son remodel his new house, the next he was so threatening that his daughter-in-law, fearful for their safety, banned him from the premises. This man—invincible in his prime—was now frail and dying from cancer. How much did a child owe to such a menacing parent? How close could he come to helping his father and not lose himself? Wertime was not a hands-on caregiver, but neither does he turn his back. The memoir chronicles the changing relationship until the day of his father's death, the first time in his life that he felt "safe."

Burton M. Wheeler, *\*Close to Me But Far Away: Living with Alzheimer's* (University of Missouri Press, 2001).

He was a retired college professor. She was a dedicated psychotherapist. Between the two of them, they understood many things—but nothing had prepared them for the greatest crisis of their married life: she developed Alzheimer's Disease while still in her sixties and he became her full time-caregiver. The memoir is structured in "a day in the life of" format. Each hour of the day is described—its particular activities and the particular thoughts they bring to the caregiver's mind. The reader is with the Wheelers from the moment they awaken until their bedtime rituals—adding an intimacy and immediacy to the narrative.

Allan Wheelis, *\*The Life and Death of My Mother* (Norton, 1992).

The memoir begins with the seventy-three-year-old author at the nursing home bedside of his hundred-year-old mother; her dying giving rise to thoughts of his own mortality. The narrative weaves back and forth from past to present. The father of the family died of tuberculosis when the author and his older sister were small children. The mother did not remarry and looked to her father, brother, and son for emotional support. Wheelis is a psychoanalyst, and both the style and substance of the memoir reflect that sensibility. Reflections upon the brutal, gratuitous killing of a pigeon Wheelis witnessed as a child recurs through the memoir, serving him as a metaphor for the pain-filled trajectory of life and its random cruelty. The mother's burial echoes that of the father and forecasts that of the author. In his vision of a beloved daughter as an old woman, the story comes full circle.

Edmund White and Hubert Sorin, *Our Paris: Sketches from Memory* (Knopf, 1995).
They met and fell in love in Paris. Both were HIV+, but it was Sorin who was ill and White who was caring for him. They decided to collaborate on a book about their life together, the places they had been, and the people they had known. White's text is a graceful evocation of daily pleasures in a Parisian household. The dog, the concierge, the gay priest, the neighborhood stores and their proprietors all rendered in glowing detail. Friends and colleagues—some of them recognizable "names"—stopped by as they pass through Paris, each giving rise to a telling observation or anecdote. The whimsical illustrations were done by Sorin on the days when he was feeling up to it. A collaborative effort to pass the long house-bound hours, this book is a powerful memorial.

C. K. Williams, *Misgivings: My Mother, My Father, Myself* (Farrar, Straus, and Giroux, 2000).
The word "misgivings" foreshadows a disquiet that pervades this memoir and reflects the author's doubts about the nature of his parents' relationship with each other and the effect of its troubling ambiguity on his own life. Williams is a poet, which may explain the structure of the book: thoughts and feelings, childhood memories and present interactions collide and reassemble as pieces of a kaleidoscope. His parents' final illnesses serve here as occasions for the author's life review rather than as care experiences in their own right. Although Williams was present during their last days (the father died of brain cancer shortly before the mother died of

lung cancer) and did what he could to make them comfortable, his is more an observational than an active role.

Sidney J. Winawer, M.D., with Nick Taylor, *Healing Lessons* (Little, Brown, 1998).

Winawer is a physician practicing in a major cancer treatment center—ironically, a specialist in the very type of cancer that attacks his wife, Andrea. As a colleague on the gastrointestinal team, he is in a privileged position to access the best medical care. Which he does— at the same time following an alternative route suggested to Andrea by her psychiatrist. These untested treatments violate everything he had ever believed about the sanctity of the scientific model; he even finds himself participating in a violation of a clinical trial protocol. With the exception of Winawer's inner conflict, his portrayal of the impact of fatal cancer on a mid-life urban couple with two teenage children is familiar. Amid the pain of losing his wife, Winawer notes that facing the challenge together enriched their marriage. And he carries the lessons he learned about the emotional needs of patients and families into his future professional work.

Marion Winik, *First Comes Love* (Vintage Books, 1996).

A straight woman falls in love with a gay man. Both are injecting heroin users. When they marry and have children, he takes on her last name and primary responsibility for the care of their two sons. When it is discovered that he has AIDS and she doesn't, the marriage enters a new phase. She is able to break free from drugs, but chronic depression as well as the tolls of the illness pull him deeper into addiction. After several incidents of domestic abuse, they separate; but she returns to care for him in his last days.

# chapter 13
## Epilogue

Animals have genes for altruism, and those genes have been selected in the evolution of many creatures because of the advantages they confer for the continuing survival of the species. . . . Altruism is based on kinship; by preserving kin, one preserves one's self.
—Lewis Thomas

Bruner (2002, 20) believes that all stories have a coda, "a retrospective evaluation of what it all might mean, a feature that also returns the hearer or reader from the there and then of the narrative to the here and now of the telling." So it is that this epilogue contains two codas: a collective one (summarizing the findings of the memoirs) and an individual one (setting out the conclusions I have drawn from the study).

## SUMMARY

What is lost is gone forever. What is gained is something else entirely. Authors find their ways along circuitous paths. Here the losses form a fog so thick that it is hard to place one foot in front of the other. Here the gains stand out in bare relief. There losses and gains are so intertwined that they are impossible to separate.

Death—occurring in many of the memoirs and haunting all the rest—is the final, but not necessarily the most devastating, of losses suffered by those who care for family members. In the case of children, siblings, or mates struck down in the prime of life, the loss is painfully deep and immutable. However, in the case of parents of advanced age or of loved ones who have experienced extreme suffering in their final illnesses, it may be viewed as inevitable, even as a relief. The death of a loved one places the author in the company of all others who mourn or have mourned. Religions and cultures have prescribed ways of responding to those who grieve—words and gestures of comfort that do not lessen the loss but provide the support of community in living through it.

Such comfort and support is seldom available to those who suffer more subtle losses: "deaths" of parts of the family member's personality long before his body is laid to rest. The mother who used to offer sage advice is now mute. The husband who is no longer the sexual partner and confidant he once was. These losses are often endured in silence—for who can complain when the one you are caring for suffers so much more? Also lost are parts of the author's identity in relation to the ill or disabled family member. No longer being a son, a mother, a wife—with all the cultural expectations and privileges attendant on the role—leaves many feeling as if a part of them has died along with their loved one.

Present losses herald future losses. Though most acutely suffered in the parents of ill or disabled children who will not grow into independent adulthood, the loss of a shared future is also keenly felt by spouses and life partners. Often there is a recognition of all that was lost in the past—opportunities that will never come again, the "unfinished business" of poor relationships that can no longer be corrected.

Present losses reawaken past losses. Memories of loved ones who have died long before are relived and lamented anew. Authors would agree with Maria Flook that "when a loss occurs, it occurs in perpetuity; it keeps regenerating like a flowering vine. What vanished once keeps vanishing, in perennial mutations" (*My Sister Life*, 12).

Other losses add to the mix: a loss of trust in a benevolent universe that does not allow bad things to happen to good people, a loss of confidence in professionals who are supposed to have the answers, a loss of reliance on institutions that claim to offer quality care. There may also be a loss of belief in one's own ability to control life's events. Authors who were used to taking charge of challenging situations and devising solutions to difficult problems often find the intractable illness or disability of a family member particularly hard to assimilate into their worldview.[1]

Moving from loss to renewal—the creation of meaning in family care—is always a work in progress. Afterwords, codas, and epilogues may provide updates on ongoing situations and new reflections on events long past. But even in their absence, the reader recognizes that the author's life goes on and that the family-care experience may have acquired new meaning in the light of subsequent events.

For every memoir of family care discussed in this book, there are many that were omitted for lack of space, many still to be published. Each tells of a family that we have never met faced with a care situation that is, in some ways, unique. Yet on the basis of the many memoirs that are included, I feel confident that these narratives will be variations on a finite set of steps from what was lost to what was gained. Not every step is taken by every author (and the steps do not necessarily occur in the same order), yet ten steps are commonly found across all family-care situations and relationships.

## Step 1: Grief and Mourning

Authors don't write to achieve "closure," "to put the past behind them," or "to get on with their lives"—the facile directives that those who have never known that depth of pain imagine are worthy goals. They write to help those who are just starting out on the road they have traveled. They write to remember—another person, themselves, and a time in their lives that seems to hold the secret of who they were and who they have become.

Anger that felt too insensitive or too risky to direct at its targets is now unleashed. Inchoate sorrow finds words. Fear, regret, self-questioning—all are a part of grieving. Scenes at the deathbed, funeral parlor, or cemetery are frequently described. Other pivotal moments include the time and place where the author first learned the family member's prognosis. The other people present, the words that were spoken, the feelings that accompanied them are portrayed in detail—the better for the reader to grasp the enormity of the author's loss. But mourning is not confined to specific occasions; it is like a dye infusing the entire narrative, dimly visible even through portrayals of happy moments. Some authors guide the newly bereaved as to what lies ahead. "Grief comes to live with us as though we'd given birth to it. And, like a baby it changes shape, size and personality, but it's ours. It's here to stay. Eventually it will come around a little less often and make less of a mess. Eventually it will only call on Sunday and holidays" (Barbara Lazear Ascher, *Landscape Without Gravity*, 55).

Often the memoir is written as a tribute to the person who has died. Pictures and reminiscences of his life fill the pages. And, in some cases, proceeds from the book's sale are devoted to organizations that advance research or provide care to those suffering from the same condition.

## Step 2: Reframing the Relationship

Mothers sometimes reject their children. Brothers sometimes treat their siblings like strangers. The relationship that exists between authors and the family members for whom they care doesn't always fit the cultural model. As a result, many memoirs have a subtext: an ongoing dialectic between the real and the ideal (i.e., the role that one's mother or brother actually played in one's life contrasted with what the author felt was "supposed" to be). When the reality of the relationship matched or exceeded the standard, reciprocity comes naturally. It seems only right that authors now provide the care they once received. They showcase their family members' virtues by describing occasions when these qualities were most in evidence. (In a few cases, they may have forgotten these or taken them for granted. Suddenly aware of a lapse of attention, they try to make up for lost time.) When the actual relationship did not live up to the ideal, authors reflect upon the reasons why, including their own responsibility for what went wrong. On the pages of their memoirs—if not in conversations with family members themselves—they ponder the causes of the damage and assess its consequences on the rest of their lives.

Often the care situation engendered an unaccustomed intimacy. Physical proximity and help with personal care (bathing, grooming, and feeding are frequently mentioned) brought many authors a new view of their ill or disabled family members. Adult children saw once invincible parents in a different light. Siblings were forced to reconsider previous assumptions they had made about brothers or sisters. Even spouses and life partners who had shared intimate moments for years spent more time together and assumed new roles in their relationships. Many authors experienced "hands-on" care as fraught with conflicting emotions: discomfort with invading the personal space of the other, compassion for the helpless state that made it necessary, reconsideration of the relationship and its place in their lives. And for those who have lived apart until a final illness or accident it is seen as a gift. "Being here is nothing less than a stroke of good luck, something I might easily never have had, this unlooked-for long visit with her before her death and while she was still alive, the time most people miss, and never get, running to deathbeds too late" (Kate Millett, *Mother Millett*, 298).

## Step 3: Separating the Illness or Disability from the Person

Traditional medicine is beginning to recognize what alternative therapies have believed for some time: that the body and the mind are inextricably linked. Even when the medical or functional problem begins as something physical, it will have mental and emotional repercussions on the life of one who suffers from it. And there are many care situations in which mental illness, instability, or deficit are primary features. Often the personality of the ill or disabled family member is profoundly affected. Children may make unrealistic demands. Adults may act out in destructive ways. Is it the illness speaking, or should they be held as responsible for inappropriate behavior as if they were well?

Back and forth the authors go—usually responding with understanding, occasionally surprising themselves with the vehemence of their anger—moments when they lose control and respond in ways that they later regret. They struggle to remember and honor the uniqueness, the essential spirit of the family member even as it erodes before their eyes. They describe in detail the times when a daughter shows undamaged parts of her personality and rejoice when parts of a father's "old self" reemerge, if even for a moment. Keeping these moments alive in their minds—as well as linking them to memories of better days—helps them to keep on.

Many authors illustrate ways in which the benign nature of family members is obscured by illness or disability. Writing of her daughter, who suffered brain trauma, Louise Ray Morningstar warns, "Because they look so normal, their different behavior comes off as even more bizarre. More often than not, they are judged to be hasty, obstinate, or drunk" (*Journey Through Brain Trauma*, 156). A few authors, however, refuse to let the illness of family members excuse their less salutatory characteristics. Emboldened by his father's weakened state, Richard Wertime is for the first time able to speak to his father of the fear he has always felt in his presence.

### Step 4: Marshaling Support

"As a nineteenth-century Hasidic rabbi once put it, 'human beings are God's language'" (Rabbi Harold Kushner, *When Bad Things Happen*, 140). All authors cite the importance of other people in helping them through the worst of times. Among the people the author depends upon are family, friends, and neighbors who were a part of his former life and a range of health-care providers and paid helpers who become crucial figures as he begins providing care.

A huge cast of characters inhabits the memoirs. Some seem archetypal figures, indistinguishable from one memoir to the next. The rushed doctor whose offhand remark causes more turmoil in the family than he could possibly imagine. The friend who discusses trivialities, unmindful of the author's troubled state of mind. Portraits of those who were unhelpful—or actually harmful—are outnumbered by those of people who are acknowledged with deep gratitude. Seeing a need and quietly filling it, offering just the right words at just the right moment are long remembered acts of kindness.

Authors frequently remark upon chance encounters that had lasting impact: the comforting hug of a nurse in the ICU, the taxi cab driver who told them his own care story. They begin to identify themselves as one of a vast underground of caregivers who recognize and give support to one another even as the rest of the world goes about its business with little recognition of what they are going through.

The longer the family member's period of illness and disability, the more likely that the people collaborating on his care (and their tasks in relation to him) will change. Authors are engaged in an ongoing process of finding, discarding, and refinding help along the way. Newfound friendships with those who are going through a similar experience provide concrete information and emotional support. Most often met through shared activities (fellow parents at a school for children with special needs, other families waiting outside the ICU), they may also be encountered in support groups.

Many authors use the memoir to pay tribute to individuals they see as unsung heroes. These individuals may have no medical training or personal connection with the family before the care situation. Some were merely acquaintances. Others were encountered by chance in the course of the care journey. Soon they became indispensable. Moonlighting from other jobs, taking time from their own lives, they are remembered with deep appreciation and undying gratitude.

## Step 5: Making Choices

Family care is never a static situation. Over time, decisions have to be made. Many are medically related to the family member's illness or disability, such as weighing the advantages and disadvantages of various interventions (invasive or noninvasive surgery, aggressive versus palliative care, mainstream versus special education classes). Some arise out of the family's desire to provide an optimum living environment for its ill or disabled member; these include weighing the comparative advantages of home and institutional care, or deciding whether it is better to move the ill or disabled family member to the author's home or have the author move in with him. Most of these choices have an effect on the author's life as well, forcing her to rethink other responsibilities and perhaps reorder her priorities.

The major decisions of family care are complicated by the fact that the person most affected by the outcome may be unable to fully participate in the process. What is more, the choice is invariably between two unappealing choices—all but ensuring negative consequences no matter what path is chosen. Authors take great pains to explain the thinking that accompanied their decisions, their efforts to involve the ill or disabled member as much as possible, the fears and questions that lingered even as the plan was under way. Looking back, they are sometimes tempted to second-guess themselves, or to express regret that they didn't choose another option; but overall, they make their peace with what can no longer be changed.

## Step 6: Pursuing Normalcy

The quotidian is never more valued than when it is threatened. It is generally accepted that work, school, and leisure activities appropriate to the ill or disabled family member's age and interests should be continued as long as possible. However, putting that philosophy into practice was difficult for the authors providing care.

The ill or disabled family member may be looked at differently by others, who are either oversolicitous or question his ability to function. Above all, he is not treated as the rest of his peers but as one set apart. Anticipating that reaction, some family members and authors delay telling others of their problems until the truth could no longer be concealed.

Even before the word is out, new ways to accomplish familiar tasks or to master new challenges are found. The family member is sometimes unrealistic about what he can continue to do and the author is torn: is this false hope that should be gently confronted or life-sustaining optimism that should be encouraged? Everyday ventures (such as dining in a restaurant, attending a concert, or visiting a friend) often involve extensive advance preparation and follow-up recuperative time. Activities that pose little or no danger to an unimpaired individual (going out in bad weather, taking a long car trip) have potentially perilous consequences for the ill or disabled family member.

Balancing between the family member's right to as normal a life as possible and one's own desire to protect him is a constant theme for authors. This is complicated by the fact that these activities usually involve extra worry, if not extra work, for the caregiver. So it is that the authors waver—now sacrificing their own concerns for the benefit of the family member, now deciding to scale back.

## Step 7: Finding Solace

Authors are most individual when it comes to finding solace to sustain them through the family-care process. Traditional or nontraditional, socially approved or condemned, they sometimes return to sources that have helped them in the past, sometimes develop new approaches.

Religion and spirituality play a role in a number of narratives. For some authors it is the ideology itself (belief in a higher power, a hereafter in which the family member will be relieved of the burdens that plague him on earth) that is the most comforting. For others, it is being part of a caring community that is provided by participation in a religious congregation.

Some authors find comfort in nature and art. Walks in the woods, in the mountains, by the shore, observing sunrises and sunsets, listening to music, reading: all quiet the mind and soothe the soul. Some authors do not seek calm but its opposite. They set themselves intellectual challenges. Others immerse themselves in the work they did before, grateful for the respite from care concerns. One solves mathematical puzzles. Several review the literature on the illness or disability from which their family member suffers, in search of more information than they receive from the professionals.

Many memoirs are howls of pain from which humor is understandably absent. But a few authors find comic relief in the ironies of the care journey and the eccentricities of those they meet along the way.

Not all sources of solace are productive. Some authors write of an excessive dependence on alcohol and prescription drugs to see them through the worst of times. Others acknowledge the satisfaction of expressions of rage directed at undeserving others. All methods of coping that were the best they could manage at the time are disowned by the memoir's end.

Many authors find comfort in keeping a written record of their experience. Some use it as a log in which to keep track of the information with which they are deluged in the course of the care experience. Others find that writing of their experience helps them reflect upon it—as well as to confide thoughts and feelings that they feel unable to share verbally with others. These journals become the spine of the memoir they eventually write.

Whatever road the authors find to solace, it is the emotional support of other people that is the greatest help. Beyond advice, beyond concrete assistance, being able to share their struggles with an understanding other is the greatest comfort of all.

## Step 8: Recognizing One's Limitations

Caring for an ill or disabled family member often plunges the author into a confrontation with parts of his nature he'd rather not face. Childhood resentments thought put to rest years before resurface with their original ardor. A feeling of being robbed and cheated of the life one expected to lead is common, sometimes resulting in an angry outburst directed against the ill or disabled family member. There may also be an irrational hatred of the well and impatience with what seem to be the pettiness of their concerns. And more than a few authors whose loved ones are terminally ill wish for their deaths to come sooner than they actually do, fantasizing about the relief of a family member's death, posing a torturing question: Are they trying to spare their family members further suffering, or do they simply want to make things easier for themselves?

There comes a time in most memoirs when the author recognizes emotionally what she has perhaps understood rationally all along: despite the best intentions and hardest efforts, she will not be able to undo or reverse the inexorable course of the family member's situation. The effect of the author's caring may make the family member more comfortable and content, may improve his quality of life, may help him use his remaining abilities to their fullest extent: but they will not save him from the fate consigned to him by his illness or disability.

If this realization can be a heartache—often marking the beginning of the mourning process—it can also be a relief. Her failure to find a way to save a loved one is no cause for self-reproach. Instead, she can set smaller goals, be satisfied with smaller achievements. And find satisfaction in what she has been able to accomplish rather than lamenting what she could not.

## *Step 9: Discovering Hidden Strengths*

Authors amaze themselves. Thrust into uncharted territory, they create their own maps. A compliant mother finds herself defying hospital authorities. A rebellious daughter finds herself admiring qualities in her parents that she previously scorned. Squeamish individuals learn how to inject needles and handle bodily fluids.

They are flexible enough to change long-standing habits, strong enough to sustain a taxing physical workload or draining emotional demands over a long period of time. They invent ways to teach the child deemed uneducable, create meals to tempt a flagging appetite, design assistive devices and techniques to help their ill or disabled family members function better. When it comes to the management of chronic illness and disability they are often able to teach the professionals a thing or two. They may also find themselves looked to as "experts" by others just beginning the care journey.

During the care situation, pride may show itself in a reluctance to take time for themselves or to accept outside help. As Molly Haskell notes, "The thought that we are enduring the unendurable is one of the things that keep us going. We become proprietary, even 'proud' of the magnitude of our disasters" (*Love and Other Infectious Diseases*, 96). They are not only smarter and stronger people than they imagined, but more giving. The experience within their own families—

and other families they come into contact with during the course of their care journey—makes them more conscious of the suffering in the world and more likely to devote time and money to health and social causes.

When the care situation ends in death, pride may be mixed with a grief that leaves them, like Mary-Lou Weisman, with "a permanent soreness and swelling about the heart . . . and the sad reassurance that it brings, like some fabled time of perfect grace, some Camelot of the spirit, the understanding that I shall never know myself to be so good again" (*Intensive Care*, 306).

## Step 10: Living in the Moment

John Bayley recalls someone named Reverend Sydney Smith of Jane Austen's time, who advised: "Take short views of human life—never further than dinner or tea" (275). In a slight variation of the theme, C. S. Lewis writes, "One never meets just Cancer, or War or Unhappiness (Or Happiness). One only meets each hour or moment that comes. All manners of ups and downs. Many bad spots in our best times, many good ones in our worst" (*A Grief Observed*, 29). For John Bayley, living in the moment means a conscious decision not to consider a future time when things would probably be worse. For C. S. Lewis, the philosophy is a retrospective appraisal of the unpredictable course of the care experience.

Care moments are endured and care moments are celebrated. Family reunions and celebrations are frequently commemorated in photographs and videos. These occasions assume a special poignancy when the ill family member is believed to be experiencing them for the last time or the functioning of a progressively disabled family member is contrasted with previous occasions when he appeared more able. But many other moments—moments that would not have been remembered, might never even have happened had the family member been well—resonate through time. A good test result, a meal successfully cooked and eaten, a walk in the park, can all be cause for celebration. A quiet afternoon with friends and family is suddenly precious. Awareness of the finiteness of life infuses everyday activities with importance. Long postponed trips or return visits to places of importance to the family member are undertaken. Celebration of the moment becomes, for many, a celebration of life itself.

Viktor Frankl, the founder of logotherapy—a method of therapy that focuses the patient toward the meaning of his life—experienced every type of loss tenfold. He was displaced from his homeland by the Holocaust and survived the horrors of a concentration camp as well as the extermination of his closest family members. What wisdom he found was this: "When we are no longer able to change a situation—we are challenged to change ourselves" ([1959, 1962] 1984, 135). Like Frankl, authors measure themselves against the demands of an unalterable situation and emerge with an altered sense of self, a changed worldview. Their own suffering opens them to the suffering of others. Life priorities are reconsidered and reordered. And one's relationships with others inevitably change. There is greater appreciation for who one's true friends are, for what one's true interests in life are, and a winnowing away of what is now seen as superfluous or unfulfilling.

At the same time, many authors are left with an unassailable sense of regret. What they could have done or should have done is belatedly recognized. Moving from their own narratives to offering advice to readers thus serves as a partial redemption. Even in the absence of regrets, authors pass on the lessons they have learned.

Authors also express gratitude to their ill and disabled family members. They recognize how difficult it often is to ask for and receive help. They reflect on the gift that their family members give them through allowing them to share their hardest days. In so doing, they acknowledge the mutuality that is an often overlooked aspect of family care. "Acceptance of help . . . is a handshake, a handhold, celebrating our mortality and our transcendence of it through kindness" (Gerda Lerner, *A Death of One's Own*, 116).

What the authors found is nothing new. It is the age-old message of philosophers, theologians, and poets: to recognize the finiteness of time and one's own place in it; to value the moments as they pass; to cherish those close to you while they live and honor their memory when they die.

Why, then, are these discoveries presented as revelations? Perhaps because they cannot be grasped intellectually but must be felt emotionally. Perhaps because their truth must be hard-earned—acquired through life rather than through literature. Yet if this were wholly the case it would be pointless to read one memoir must less analyze over one hundred. So it must be that imaginatively entering the emotional life of a family—through reading the narrative of the author—provides a lived experience of another sort. The experience of another that resonates with, and enriches, our own.

## Conclusion

In the decade since I began reading family-care memoirs, the field of narrative medicine has come into its own. This welcome development is due in no small part to the efforts of Maura Spiegel and Rita Charon (2004, ix), editors-in-chief of *Literature and Medicine*. Through that journal and sponsorship of related conferences that unite several fields of scholarship, they have directed overdue attention to differences between the patient's view and that of the professionals who care for him. In many ways and many contexts, they have considered—and inspired others to consider—the question of narrative's practical impact on the field of medicine.

My reading of memoirs suggests that caregiver narratives can and should join patient narratives in influencing the practice of medicine as well as allied health-care fields. In fact, Dennis Saleebey has directly tied the study of narrative to the purposes of social work. His words apply to other helping professionals as well: "Practitioners need to know how meaning . . . affects intention and action, feeling and mood, relationships, interactions with the surrounding world, well-being, and possibility. They also need to know how meaning can get people into trouble, get them stuck, or embroil them in crisis. . . . So meaning, dependent on its context, symbolic nature, and nature, can inspire or oppress" (1994, 357).

The meanings that caregivers ascribe to their experience belong to a category that Foucault (1976, 82) would term "naïve knowledges located low-down on the hierarchy, beneath the required level of cognition and scientificy" that hold power if we but recognize them. The existence of what he termed "subjugated" knowledge and populations was not news to social worker practitioners, theorists, or researchers. Nor was the importance of giving them voice. Hartman (1990, 1992), Chambon, Irving, and Epstein (1999), and Gorman (1993) have since made compelling cases for the heuristic and social value of client stories.

What I sought in narrative was expansion of the received wisdom on family care. I wanted to go beyond the quantitative data that linked demographic characteristics and caregiving tasks with measures of stress and burden. I wanted to better understand the process—how it evolved over time and what meaning those who cared for ill or disabled family members took from the experience. What I found was that the story of family care is more than the sum of its parts. Cultural associations of the illness or disability—what David Shenk calls "the flavor of the name"—affected how the care process was experienced. Each of the four care situations most frequently chronicled (cancer, mental illness/addiction, HIV/AIDS, and dementia) had its own trajectory. The presence or absence of stigma or blame; the length of time the situation continued, the number and effectiveness of treatments and interventions; the availability and use of concrete and emotional support from health-care providers all contributed to the meaning family members took from the experience.

Cultural views on what it means to be a parent, a life partner, a sibling, a child—and the responsibilities and expectations arising from each relationship—were equally influential. The meanings that the authors extracted from the family-care experience—though based on the shared history and unique characteristics of those involved—drew on these sources and were inextricably bound to them.

The synergistic effects of care situation, care relationship, and individual variations cannot be disentangled for easy study. However, the validity of the ten steps I identify as marking the path from what family care members lost to what they found lend themselves to further inquiry. Longitudinal studies of family care are obviously difficult to fund or conduct. However, researchers could direct attention to the retrospective meaning of the experience one, five, or ten years after it is over. Whether they are testing hypotheses suggested in this study or exploring new avenues on their own—such research would open avenues for consideration.

The issue of friend care—mentioned briefly in this book—is worthy of future study. The few memoirs in this section suggest significant similarities and differences with family care. As many adults now live at a distance from their families of origin and have not established families of their own, a better understanding of the limits and possibilities of friend caring for friend would have important policy and practice implications.

The four care situations discussed in this book were the most commonly found in the memoirs I read. As the memoir literature increases, however, there are other illnesses and disabilities represented—autism, developmental disabilities, and accidents among them. Based on the findings of this study, it is possible that they too have a typical trajectory that could be unearthed by narrative analysis.

A last, and most important, area for future study are the memoirs of the recipients of family care—ill and disabled people themselves. There are a great number of these memoirs in print; seeing how they agree with or contradict the findings of family care memoirs would be a fascinating study.

For the clinician, memoirs offer a treasure trove of possibility. Memoirs can be recommended to clients who are receiving or providing care—joining them to others in the same situation. (This can be especially useful for individuals who feel isolated in their experience yet lack access to or are unwilling to participate in a support group.)Memoirs suggest areas to be explored when family members first approach clinicians for help. In fact, it is impossible to read of authors' experiences without realizing the inadequacy of the usual methods of gathering information. Forms that collect data on how the ill or disabled person accomplishes activities of daily living are frequently called "assessments" but rarely devote more than a few lines to the family members involved in their care. And it is never suggested that the past history of the family and the meanings that its members attach to the experience are worthy of inquiry or exploration. Or that the effective delivery of concrete services to families is dependent on an understanding of their motivations and beliefs.

Clinicians may be startled to read that the practice wisdom that guides many traditional interventions is at odds with the way family caregivers perceive their situation. For example, the advice to "take time for yourself" will not be heeded if the caregiver—as many of the authors—takes pride in how much stress she can endure. And suggestions that the family make plans for the future may not recognize how much strength caregivers find living in the present. Memoirs are a reminder that any professional advice must be tailored to the individual to whom it is directed; and that knowledge of the individual can be acquired only through explorations of the meaning of the experience to him.

For the reader who has gone through a family-care experience, the memoir becomes a source of comparison. How do the author's reactions resemble her own? Did she make the same choices, come to the same conclusions, in a similar situation? The reader may find a confirmation of her own beliefs or come upon an interpretation so different that she is forced to reconsider. For those who are currently in the throes of a family-care experience, a memoir that depicts the same situation or relationship is more than reassurance that someone has survived to tell the tale—it provides a picture of the care career that is rarely seen in the popular media. (For unlike marriage, child-rearing, or work careers, which are well-documented, family care is portrayed—if at all—as an acute, time-limited activity.)

Memoirs of family care offer a variety of practical suggestions as well as emotional support. Most of all, they alert readers to the fact that what they are going through today will look a lot different a year, five years, or ten years from now. Projecting themselves into that future time and looking back at the present moment may provide a helpful, comforting perspective.

Three questions have dogged me throughout the reading of the memoirs and the writing of this book. Provocative, unresolved, I raise them here for the reader's consideration.

## Question 1: Is It Useful to Make a Distinction Between Family Caregiving and Family Caring?

The term "family caregiving" (concrete help with the activities of daily living) has been coined, defined, and owned by those who wish to differentiate the demands of caring for an ill or disabled relative from the relationship that would exist if the family member were more independent. "Family caring" may be defined as emotional attachment to an ill or disabled relative that does not include hands-on involvement.

There are many benefits to be gained by privileging "family caregiving" bestowing a superior status on those who practice it. Recognition from the government, health-care providers, and the individual caregivers themselves that they have legitimate needs for money, services, and social support; that they are engaged in activities above and beyond what one usually associates with the family roles of parent, child, sibling, life partner, or spouse. The family caregiving movement also provides a language and a job description in which those who spend large amounts of time in the activity can communicate, feel pride, and receive recognition for their efforts.

An unfortunate—and probably unforeseen—consequence of the term is that it has removed the provision of care to ill or disabled relatives from being an inevitable part of the human condition to a state apart, an interruption of "real life." Further, in its focus on primary caregivers, little or no attention is paid to other family members. Many of the authors did not provide hands-on care; a few did little more than observe from afar. Yet the illness or disability of their relatives affected them profoundly—having a transformative effect on their lives.

Family caregivers who devote days and nights to the physical care of their loved ones, often at great financial and personal cost to themselves, might well object to having recognition accorded to those who have not exerted that effort. On the other hand, extending the notion of family care beyond the hands-on caregiver would more accurately reflect the message of the memoirs. Family caring for ill and disabled loved ones could then become as commonly portrayed in the media and in public discourse as the vast number of people involved in the activity would warrant. In short, the problem is not semantic but conceptual. And has no easy answer.

## *Question 2: When Do Differences Make a Difference?*

Age, gender, race, ethnicity, education, income, social class, religion, language, sexual orientation, and geographical location are all caregiver characteristics that are widely studied in quantitative research. The memoirs do not lend themselves to an analysis of these variables, since their authors are self-selected and less diverse than the general population. However, in the areas in which there is diversity—age and gender—there are some findings that catch the eye without immediately yielding their import. For example, men are just as likely to write about the care experience as women but less likely to perform hands-on care. Is this simply a reflection of traditional gender roles or is something less obvious afoot?

Similarly, although authors range in age from their early twenties to mid seventies, with most clustering in the middle years (very much like a bell curve), their reactions to the care experience do not differ as much as theories of life-stage development might lead one to think. Since the authors are a cultural elite—with more educational and financial assets—than the general public, it might suggest that resources trump age in determining the nature of the experience for an individual caregiver. This, too, is open to question.

## *3. Do People Who Don't Write Memoirs Derive the Same Meanings from the Family-care Experience as People Who Do?*

The process of writing forces authors to remember, reflect, and come to some conclusions about what the experience meant to them. As Michel de Montaigne famously observed, "Painting myself for others, I have painted my inward self with colors clearer than my original ones. I have no more made my book than my book has made me" (cited in Watson 1993, 63). The authors' conclusions often resonate with their readers, inspiring them to reflect upon their own situations—and come up with their own meanings.

But what of those who neither read nor write memoirs? Clinical practice suggests that they, too, have stories to tell and may benefit others and themselves from doing so in oral or written form. It would be interesting to discover whether they would find the process of remembering, reflecting, and coming to conclusions as useful in creating meaning out of the family-care experience as the memoir authors did. In fact, Philippe Lejeune concludes a literary treatise on autobiography with a chapter entitled "Teaching People to Write Their Life Story" (1989).[2]

The study is over; the memoirs on my bookshelves remain. A fluid categorizing system—now by situation, now by relationship, now by year of publication—has given way to a straightforward alphabetical procession. Annotated, underlined, dog-eared, they have earned a permanent place in my psychic as well as physical life. As I scan the spines, remembering an anecdote from one, a photograph from another, a particular turn of phrase from a third, it is a comfort to see them there—concrete reminders of the depth, capacity, and resilience of the human spirit.

# appendix 1

## The Memoirs,

### by Care Relationship and Care Situation

**RELATIONSHIP STORY**
CHILD
SIBLING
FRIEND
LIFE PARTNER/SPOUSE
PARENT

**INDIVIDUAL STORY**

**SITUATION STORY**
HIV/AIDS
CANCER
DEMENTIA
MENTAL ILLNESS
CHEMICAL DEPENDENCY

CHILD CARE

| | Cancer | Mental Illness/ Chemical Dependence | HIV/AIDS | Developmental Delays/ Autism | Accident | Genetic/ Acquired Disease/ Other |
|---|---|---|---|---|---|---|
| J. J. Allen | | | X | | | |
| I. Allende | | | | | | X |
| M. Beck | | | | X | | |
| J. Bernstein | | | | X | | |
| M. Berube | | | | X | | |
| D. L. Breen | X | | | | | |
| K. Brennan | | | | | X | |
| P. and H. Broadbent | | | X | | | |
| A. Colin | | | | X | | |
| D. R. Collins | | | | | | X |
| E. K. Davis | | | | | | X |
| H. C. Davis | X | | | | | |
| M. Dorris | | | | X | | |
| M. T. Dudman | | X | | | | |
| B. and J. Ellison | | | | | X | |
| R. R. Galli | | | | | X | |
| E. Glaser | | | X | | | |

| | Cancer | Mental Illness/Chemical Dependence | HIV/AIDS | Developmental Delays/Autism | Accident | Genetic/Acquired Disease/Other |
|---|---|---|---|---|---|---|
| J. Gunther | X | | | | | |
| M. Jablow | | | | X | | |
| L. S. Kramer | | | | | | X |
| H. Kushner | | | | | | X |
| M. Lehmann | | | | | X | |
| G. Livingston | X | | | | | |
| D. Lund | X | | | | | |
| J. T. McDonnell | | | | X | | |
| G. McGovern | | X | | | | |
| L. R. Morningstar | | | | | X | |
| K. Oë | | | | X | | X |
| C. C. Park | | | | X | | |
| J. L. Richards | | | | | | X |
| D. Steele | | X | | | | |
| G. Vanderbilt | | X | | | | |
| M. L. Weisman | | | | | | X |

COUPLE CARE

| | Cancer | Dementia | HIV/AIDS | Neurological Disease | Heart Disease | Other |
|---|---|---|---|---|---|---|
| A. Alterra | | X | | | | |
| J. Bayley | | X | | | | |
| S. Broyard | X | | | | | |
| J. A. Burns | | | X | | | |
| E. Cox | | | X | | | |
| J. Craig | X | | | | | |
| L. Elmer | X | | | | | |
| J. Gould | X | | | | | |
| D. Hall | X | | | | | |
| M. Haskell | | | | | | X |
| F. Johnson | | | X | | | |
| M. Kondrake | | | | X | | |
| M. W. Lear | | | | | X | |
| G. Lerner | X | | | | | |

| | Cancer | Dementia | HIV/AIDS | Neurological Disease | Heart Disease | Other |
|---|---|---|---|---|---|---|
| R. Levin | | | | | X | |
| C. S. Lewis | X | | | | | |
| P. Linke | X | | | | | |
| S. Mack | X | | | | | |
| G. Manning | | | | | | X |
| P. Monette | | | X | | | |
| B. B. Murphy | | X | | | | |
| N. Rossi | X | | | | | |
| M. Strong | | | | X | | |
| B. M. Wheeler | | X | | | | |
| E. White | | | X | | | |
| S. J. Winawer | X | | | | | |
| M. Winik | | | X | | | |

## SIBLING CARE

|  | Cancer | Mental Illness/Chemical Dependence | HIV/AIDS | Developmental Delays | Accident |
|---|---|---|---|---|---|
| B. L. Ascher |  |  | X |  |  |
| G. Bottoms |  | X |  |  |  |
| C. Chase |  |  | X |  |  |
| J. D. Dolan |  |  |  |  | X |
| M. Flook |  | X |  |  |  |
| J. Kincaid |  |  | X |  |  |
| M. Moorman |  | X |  |  |  |
| J. Neugeboren |  | X |  |  |  |
| A. Shapiro | X |  |  |  |  |
| R. Simon |  |  |  | X |  |
| B. Smith |  |  |  | X |  |
| E. Swados |  | X |  |  |  |

## FRIEND CARE

|  | Cancer | Mental Illness/Chemical Dependence | HIV/AIDS | Neurological Disease |
|---|---|---|---|---|
| J. Heller and S. Vogel |  |  |  | X |
| A. Hoffman |  |  | X |  |
| T. R. McGee | X |  |  |  |
| A. Patchett | X | X |  |  |
| C. Trillin |  | X |  |  |
| A. Verghese |  | X |  |  |

PARENT CARE

| | Cancer | Mental Illness/ Chemical Dependence | HIV/AIDS | Dementia | Accident | Neurological/ Sensory Loss | Heart/ Stroke |
|---|---|---|---|---|---|---|---|
| M. Amis | | X | | X | | | |
| B. Avadian | | | | X | | | |
| S. Bergman | | | X | | | | |
| I. Brautigan | | X | | | | | |
| B. M. Campbell | | | | | X | | |
| S. Cheever | X | X | | | | | |
| E. Cooney | | | | X | | | |
| L. J. Davis | | | | | | X | |
| S. de Beauvoir | X | | | | | | |
| C. Dickey | | X | | | | | |
| D. Eggers | X | | | | | | |
| A. Ernaux | | | | X | | | |
| M. Gordon | | | | X | | | |
| J. Gould | | | | | | | X |
| J. F. Graham | X | | | | | | |
| L. Grant | | | | X | | | |
| J. Hilden | | X | | X | | | |

PARENT CARE (CONTINUED)

| | Cancer | Mental Illness/ Chemical Dependence | HIV/AIDS | Dementia | Accident | Neurological/ Sensory Loss | Heart/ Stroke |
|---|---|---|---|---|---|---|---|
| T. E. Holley | | X | | | | | |
| A. Hood | X | | | | | | |
| H. Johnson | X | | | | | | |
| R. Kamenetz | X | | | | | | |
| K. Karbo | X | | | | | | |
| N. Lachenmeyer | | X | | | | | |
| M. L'Engle | | | | X | | | |
| R. Lindbergh | | | | X | | | |
| J. Lyden | | X | | | | | |
| A. H. Malcolm | X | | | | | | |
| S. Miller | | | | X | | | |
| K. Millet | X | | | | | | |
| S. B. Nuland | | | | | | X | |
| C. P. Pierce | | | | X | | | |
| J. Reibstein | X | | | | | | |
| M. Roach | | | | X | | | |

PARENT CARE (CONTINUED)

| | Cancer | Mental Illness/ Chemical Dependence | HIV/AIDS | Dementia | Accident | Neurological/ Sensory Loss | Heart/ Stroke |
|---|---|---|---|---|---|---|---|
| B. Rollin | X | | | | | | |
| P. Roth | X | | | | | | |
| R. Rozelle | | | | X | | | |
| D. Rubin | X | | | | | | X |
| L. B. Rubin | | | | X | | | |
| L. Schreiber | X | | | | | | |
| D. Shapiro | | | | | X | | |
| T. M. Shine | | | | | | | X |
| A. K. Shulman | | | | X | | | X |
| T. Solotaroff | | | | | | | X |
| E. Swados | | X | | | | | |
| C. Trillin | | | | | | | X |
| L. A. Walker | | | | | | X | |
| R. Wertime | X | | | | | | |
| A. Wheelis | | | | X | | | |
| C. K. Williams | X | | | | | | X |

# Notes

*'Crystallized Love'"*

1. Families have always looked after their own. But it was not until the last decades of the twentieth century—when the consequences of medical and technological advances first entered public awareness—that someone who helped an ailing relative was deemed worthy of a title: "family caregiver." Many illnesses that were previously fatal could now be treated (if not yet cured). Many disabilities that had previously landed their sufferers in institutions were now being managed at home. The elderly were the largest, but by no means the only, age group affected. Developments in pediatric medicine, long-term survivorship with cancer and HIV/AIDS, and improved management of chronic illnesses touched everyone. Few areas of contemporary life received more research, programmatic, or advocacy attention.

Large-scale studies—over a span of four decades—confirmed a few basic truths. Families rarely appealed to outsiders for help until their own resources were exhausted; relatives did not necessarily have to share a household or neighborhood to be caregivers; care passed between the generations throughout the lifespan (moving from older to younger in the early years and reversing in the later years); ethnic and cultural differences influenced many aspects of the process but not the essential nature of the family-caring response. Above all, caring exacted a price from all who provided it. If the financial consequences of providing care to family members could be measured in lost workdays and out-of-pocket expenses, emotional costs were no less evident. "Stress" and "burden" were linked to specific characteristics of caregiver, patient, and illness.

Needs assessments and service utilization studies investigated the ways in which outside services meshed with the needs of patients and their families. Positive outcomes were rarely recognized. Appearing under the rubric of "adaptation" or "coping," a few studies addressed the strengths that caregivers employed to meet the challenge. Fewer still identified difficult situations as "hassles" and pleasant ones as "uplifts," so acknowledging that caregiving need not be an unremitting nightmare. However, their voices were all but drowned out in the dominant paradigm.

2. "Personal tasks of daily living" include assistance with bathing, feeding, toileting, and other intimate activities. "Instrumental tasks" include assistance with marketing, finances, transportation, and other activities that the relative may no longer be able to perform independently.

3. Of the more than one hundred memoirs I eventually read, the subjects of about a dozen did not meet the traditional criteria of "family": those bound by blood or marriage. Life partners, adopted children, friends—their stories extended and enriched the definition.

4. Each chapter could easily be expanded to fill a book of its own. Viewing the shared story of a particular relationship or situation through a variety of lenses (culture, gender, class, age) would generate useful insights.

5. In selecting the memoirs, I felt there were a few classics of decades past that could not be ignored (for example, John Gunther's *Death Be Not Proud* and Simone de Beauvoir's *A Very Easy Death*). Most, however, were published after 1990 and so reflect recent trends in medical, psychiatric, and rehabilitative care. The majority are still in print, and even that aren't can be accessed through libraries, bookstores, and the Internet.

### 1. "Introduction: 'The Flavor of the Name'"

1. Some of the unexpectedness of the family-care experience may have to do with popular culture. The images of family life portrayed in the media rarely reflect the reality of millions of families. And when such a situation is shown—a daughter in a wheelchair after an accident, a husband who is unable to speak clearly after a stroke—the illness or disability is always the main point of the story. Slowly this is changing. (The inclusion of people with visible health problems is evident in some commercials.) But until it becomes commonplace, individuals will continue to be shocked when what is perceived to be a rare situation actually happens to them.

2. Professionals refer to the former as the "formal system" and the latter as the "informal system." Put another way, there are those who arrive on the scene as a result of the relative's difficulties and those who were

there before. Sometimes there are crossovers—the doctor or home health aide who becomes "one of the family," the old friend who happens to be a nurse. However, the primary distinction is that those who are paid to care have assigned tasks.

3. Using a quantitative approach, Biegel, Sales, and Shulz (1991) identified illness- distinct variables in Alzheimer's Disease, cancer, mental illness, and stroke.

## 2. *"Cancer: Cancer's Gift"*

1. Using cancer as a case in point, Kübler-Ross posited a series of stages through which patients (as well as the bereaved) must pass in dealing with terminal illness. The stages are shock and disbelief, denial, anger, bargaining, sadness, and acceptance.

## 5. *"Mental Illness/Chemical Dependence: 'Companion Demons' "*

1. The 1970s were a time of great change in the way mental health and chemical dependence services were delivered. The efficacy of newly developed psychotropic medications led to the belief that many institutionalized people could be sufficiently stabilized to live on their own. The problem was that community mental health and social services could not keep pace with the number and needs of patients, many of whom were now ricocheting from one bad situation to another. The fact that many of these patients did not see themselves as ill and soon discontinued taking prescribed medications, or began self-medicating with the illegal drugs then flooding the streets, was not anticipated. Nor were the vast challenges they faced in keeping themselves fed, clothed, and housed while struggling with an altered sense of reality. There were also changes in the philosophy of care. Shifting power from institutions to the people they served sounded good. Self-help and rehabilitation programs that focused on personal efficacy and responsibility were seen as more democratic and in keeping with the prevailing Zeitgeist. However, these worthy goals were not backed up with services. The fine line between independence from the system and abandonment by it was—and remains—hard to distinguish.

## 7. *"Child Care: 'An Unimagined Life' "*

1. These and other pioneering parents were very much a product of their time in history—a time when a confluence of biomedical research,

technological advances, and cultural change made it easier for their children to find their places in the world.

### 8. "Sibling Care: 'She Was My Parents' Child, and So Was I'"

1. Perhaps it has been ever thus. Contrast the oft-quoted Biblical question: "Am I my brother's keeper?" to the commandment "Honor they father and thy mother." At least two authors have answered the question in the affirmative, turning the question into a book title: Margaret Moorman in *My Sister's Keeper* and John Edgar Wideman, writing of a sibling in jail, *Brothers and Keepers* (New York, Vintage Books, 1984).

2. All of the authors who grow up with impaired siblings are faced with cognitively and emotionally disabled brothers and sisters. Most likely the situation would be quite different if their siblings were physically disabled and mentally competent to make decisions for themselves.

### 10. "Parent Care: 'The Consummate Act'"

1. There are more memoirs of the parent-care experience than of any other—perhaps because the category includes books that are not specifically written to discuss the experience but inevitably include it (for whatever an author's purpose in writing an autobiography, the relationship with parents up to their final illness and death is an integral part of the story). Sometimes—as in the case of Phillip Roth or Simone de Beauvoir—the memoir is devoted to the parent, but it is the promise of learning more about the life of the celebrated child that commands initial attention. Sometimes the author has followed in the parent's literary footsteps: Martin Amis and Kingsley Amis, Christopher Dickey and James Dickey, Susan Cheever and John Cheever, Reeve Lindbergh and Anne Morrow Lindbergh. Part biography of a person the world wants to know more about, part memoir of a child emerging from the shadow of a celebrated parent, these stories of parent care combine many powerful themes.

Most memoirs, however, are written by and about unfamiliar people involved in familiar situations: a parent's end-of-life struggle with cancer or dementia being the most common.

### 11. "Introduction: 'Jointly Human'"

1. Issues of "reference and temporal order" in the construction and understanding of stories are covered extensively in the literature of life history and narrative.

## 13. Epilogue

1. This aspect might reflect the demographic profile of the authors, most of whom are privileged by education and income.

2. Lejeune suggests a way to prompt people to tell life stories: " 'Could you talk to me about your given name and your last name? What do they remind you of?' Experience shows that this is an inexhaustible question, and an absolutely central one. Dear reader, it's up to you to answer it. What is your name?" (1989, 231).

# Sources Cited

Adams, Timothy Dow. 2000. *Light Writing and Life Writing: Photography in Autobiography*. Chapel Hill: University of North Carolina Press.

Biegel, David E., Esther Sales, and Richard Schulz. 1991. *Family Caregiving in Chronic Illness: Alzheimer's Disease, Cancer, Mental Illness, and Stroke*. Newbury Park, Calif.: Sage Publications.

Brody, Harold. 1987. *Stories of Sickness*. New Haven: Yale University Press.

Bruner, Jerome. 1993. "The Autobiographical Process." In R. Folkenflik, ed., *The Culture of Autobiography: Constructions of Self-Representation*, 38–56. Stanford: Stanford University Press.

———. 2001. *Making Stories: Law, Literature, Life*. New York: Farrar, Straus, and Giroux.

Buchanan, James H. 1989. *Patient Encounters: The Experience of Disease*. New York: Henry Holt and Company.

Burack-Weiss, Ann. 1995. "The Caregiver's Memoir: A New Look at Family Support." *Social Work* 40: 391–396.

Chambon, Adrienne S., Allan Irving, and Laura Epstein, eds. 1999. *Reading Foucault for Social Work*. New York: Columbia University Press.

Coles, Robert. 1989. *The Call of Stories: Teaching and the Moral Imagination*. Boston: Houghton Mifflin.

Couser, G. Thomas. 1997. *Recovering Bodies: Illness, Disability, and Life Writing*. Madison: University of Wisconsin Press.

Dossey, Larry. 1991. *Meaning and Medicine: Lessons from a Doctor's Tales of Breakthrough and Healing*. New York: Bantam Books.

Foucault, Michel. 1972–1977. *Selected Interviews and Other Writings*, ed. C. Gordon. New York: Pantheon Books.

Frank, Arthur W. 1995. *The Wounded Storyteller: Body, Illness, and Ethics*. Chicago: University of Chicago Press.

Frankl, Viktor. (1959, 1962) 1984. *Man's Search for Meaning*. New York: Simon and Schuster.

Gass, William. 1994. "The Art of Self: Autobiography in an Age of Narcissism." *Harpers* (May), 43–52.

Gaylin, William. 1976. *Caring*. New York: Knopf.

Gorman, J. 1993. "Postmodernism and the Conduct of Inquiry in Social Work." *Affilia* 8: 247–262.

Gornick, Vivian. 2002. *The Situation and the Story*. New York: Farrar, Straus, and Giroux.

Hartman, Ann. 1990. "Many Ways of Knowing." *Social Work* 35: 3–4.

———. 1992. "In Search of Subjugated Knowledge." *Social Work* 37: 483–484.

Hawkins, Anne Hunsaker. 1993, 1999. *Reconstructing Illness: Studies in Pathography*. West Lafayette, Indiana: Purdue University Press.

Kleinman, Arthur. 1998. *The Illness Narratives*. New York: Basic Books.

Kübler-Ross, Elisabeth. 1969. *On Death and Dying*. New York: Macmillan.

Leibowitz, Herbert. 1989. *Fabricating Lives: Explorations in American Autobiography*. New York: Knopf.

Lejeune, Philippe. 1989. *On Autobiography*. Minneapolis: University of Minnesota Press.

Levi-Strauss, C. 1966. *The Savage Mind*. 2d ed. Chicago: University of Chicago Press.

Mishler, Elliot G. 1995. "Models of Narrative Analysis: A Typology." *Journal of Narrative and Life History* 5: 87–123.

Olney, James. 1998. *Memory and Narrative: The Weave of Life-Writing*. Chicago: University of Chicago Press.

Saleebey, Dennis. 1994. "Culture, Theory, and Narrative: The Intersection of Meanings in Practice." *Social Work* 39: 351–359.

Shenk, David. 2001. *The Forgetting*. New York: Random House.

Sontag, Susan. 1978. *Illness as Metaphor*. New York: Farrar, Straus, and Giroux.

———. 1989. *AIDS and Its Metaphors*. New York: Farrar, Straus, and Giroux.

Spiegel, Marua, and Rita Charon. 2004. "Editors' Preface: Narrative, Empathy, Proximity." *Literature and Medicine* 23: xiii.

Thomas, Lewis. 1980. *Late Night Thoughts on Listening to Mahler's Ninth Symphony*. New York: Viking.

Watson, Julia. 1993. "Toward an Anti-Metaphysics of Autobiography." In R. Folkenflik, ed., *The Culture of Autobiography: Constructions of Self-Representation*, 56–79. Stanford: Stanford University Press.

Weinstein, D., and M. A. Weinstein. 1991. "George Simmel: Sociological Flaneur Bricoleur." *Theory, Culture, and Society* 8: 161.

Welty, Eudora. 1983, 1984. *One Writer's Beginnings*. New York: Warner Books

## Of Further Interest

Bateson, Mary Catherine. 1990. *Composing a Life*. New York: Penguin Books.

Bruner, Jerome. 1987. "Life as Narrative." *Social Research* 54: 11–32.

Denzin, Norman K., and Yvonna S. Lincoln, eds. 1998. *Collecting and Interpreting Qualitative Materials*. Thousand Oaks, Calif.: Sage Publications.

Levine, Carol, ed. 2000. *Always on Call: When Illness Turns Families Into Caregivers*. United Hospital Fund of New York.

Nuland, Sharon B. 1993. *How We Die: Reflections on Life's Final Chapter*. New York: Vintage Books.

Riessman, Catherine Kohler. 1993. *Narrative Analysis*. Newbury Park, Calif.: Sage Publications.

White, Michael, and David Epstein. 1990. *Narrative Means to Therapeutic Ends*. New York: Norton.

Zinsser, William. 1995. *Inventing the Truth: The Art and Craft of Memoir*. Boston: Houghton Mifflin.

# Index